DISCARD

What I Learned

from

Jackie Robinson

ALSO BY CARL ERSKINE

Carl Erskine's Tales from the Dodgers' Dugout: Extra Innings

ALSO BY BURTON ROCKS

Me and My Dad: A Baseball Memoir (with Paul O'Neill)

Bob Feller's Little Black Book of Baseball Wisdom (with Bob Feller)

A King's Legacy: The Clyde King Story (with Clyde King)

The Long and Short of It (with Andy North)

What I Learned

from

Jackie Robinson

A TEAMMATE'S REFLECTIONS
ON AND OFF THE FIELD

Carl Erskine

with Burton Rocks

McGraw·Hill

New York   Chicago   San Francisco   Lisbon   London   Madrid   Mexico City
Milan   New Delhi   San Juan   Seoul   Singapore   Sydney   Toronto

Library of Congress Cataloging-in-Publication Data

Erskine, Carl.
  What I learned from Jackie Robinson : a teammate's reflections on and off the field / by Carl Erskine with Burton Rocks.
      p.   cm.
  ISBN 0-07-145085-8
      1. Robinson, Jackie, 1919–1972.   2. Baseball players—United States—Biography.   3. Erskine, Carl—Friends and associates.   4. Brooklyn Dodgers (Baseball team)—History.   I. Rocks, Burton.   II. Title.

  GV865.R6 E77   2005
  796.357'092—dc22
                                                          2004024980

1 2 3 4 5 6 7 8 9 0   FGR/FGR   0 9 8 7 6 5

ISBN 0-07-145085-8

Interior photographs are courtesy of the author unless otherwise noted.

McGraw-Hill books are available at special quantity discounts to use as premiums and sales promotions, or for use in corporate training programs. For more information, please write to the Director of Special Sales, Professional Publishing, McGraw-Hill, Two Penn Plaza, New York, NY 10121-2298. Or contact your local bookstore.

This book is printed on acid-free paper.

This book is dedicated to two unique women,
Rachel Robinson and Betty Erskine,
for their love, dedication, strength, and perseverance
in the journey to see Jackie and Jimmy succeed.

Contents

Foreword

I MET CARL ERSKINE WHEN WE both were minor-league prospects in that huge Dodgers farm system, leapfrogging to the majors. We became instant friends and roomed together in the big leagues. For well over a decade we fought the fires, in both personal challenges and team stresses, and became brothers without the blood.

I saw Jackie Robinson before he entered the game of baseball, while he was a star athlete at UCLA, excelling in four different sports—he was, and still is, the only four-sport letterman ever at UCLA. Ironically, baseball was not his strongest sport, but baseball did offer the perfect stage for Branch Rickey to present Jackie Robinson to the world.

These two teammates, Carl and Jackie, had a special rapport. They had, and have, a real story to tell. My locker was located right across from Jackie's, and reading this book makes me think back to the times he came into that locker room, his game face on and his competitive spirit showing. Jackie was out to prove on and off the diamond that racial equality was long overdue; his role was to help the Dodgers win on a daily basis, but the bigger goal was gaining self-respect for his people and assuring the dignity of every individual.

Carl and Betty's challenges were also social ones, challenges with their Down syndrome son, Jimmy, that affected them after Carl had left the game. Many of the barriers they faced with

Jimmy were much like Jackie's: tradition, superstition, ignorance, fear, and general acceptance.

Carl and Burton have told a compelling story—an eyewitness account by a teammate and a father of two of the greatest social changes of the twentieth century.

—Duke Snider

Acknowledgments

WE ARE GRATEFUL TO Bill Adler, our literary agent, who shepherded us every step of the way, and right to the desk of Mark Weinstein at McGraw-Hill. Mark, we thank you for your heartfelt enthusiasm, patience, and outstanding editing of this book. A hearty thanks to Craig Bolt and to Beth Tarson at McGraw-Hill as well for their efforts in making this book a success. To have a foreword from the Duke of Flatbush is indeed an honor; Duke, we thank you so very much for your foreword and your encouragement! Tommy Lasorda, a teammate of Jackie's, we thank for the quote for this book! We wish to thank Mark Langill at the Los Angeles Dodgers, the Dodgers organization, and the National Baseball Hall of Fame for their efforts in helping us with important photographs for this book, as well as friends and family along the way for emotional support.

"A life is not important except in the impact it makes on other lives."

—Jackie Robinson

1

The Robinson Way

JACKIE ROBINSON BROKE BARRIERS far beyond those demarked by race and ethnicity. He changed the way Americans viewed themselves and each other. His genius was that he did it in the most subliminal manner, through the game everyone called their national pastime, by questioning how a national pastime could not be equal to all.

It was as if every time Jackie stole home, hit a bullet home run, or turned the double play with Pee Wee Reese, another barrier came down. In retrospect, a man on a diamond forced Americans to look into the mirror and inside their own soul.

Civil rights legislation, championed by Jackie, also led to a massive legislative effort to afford handicapped individuals rights they had not been previously afforded. His impact on society through baseball enabled America—and the game of baseball—to rejuvenate itself in ways that were not imagined prior to World War II.

And so, fifty years after the Dodgers won it all in 1955, a young man named Jimmy Erskine from Anderson, Indiana, with Down syndrome has a gold medal from the Special Olympics on his wall—all because way back in 1947 a brave young man stood up to America for the America that he so passionately loved.

If someone would have told me growing up in Anderson, Indiana, that Jackie Robinson would have sought me out—a minor-league kid—to give me encouragement one humid day in March 1948 in sunny Fort Worth, Texas, I would never have believed it.

Of all the things that have happened to me in this wonderful game of baseball, that day when Jackie came over to me is atop the list.

It seems rather prophetic to me now when I sit back in my den and remember my baseball roots and the fact that it all began in Brooklyn, New York. Who would have ever thought that 215 Montague Street would be home to the likes of Pee Wee Reese, Jackie Robinson, and me? But this reporting address was the same for me as it was for all of the great players who preceded me.

Brooklyn was where swelling crowds of thirty-four thousand were daily living and breathing American history while taking in hot dogs and Cracker Jack back in 1947. No more perfect a place existed than Brooklyn for the type of social transformation that Robinson would lead. I hadn't realized the true melting-pot attitude of the community—Bay Ridge, Brighton Beach, Coney Island, Bensonhurst—until I became fully entrenched with the team. But by the end of 1948 it was apparent that these fans loved their team and loved each other. I don't think the fans realized at the time just how much they meant to the civil rights movement.

Although I was not an eyewitness to the events at Ebbets Field on April 15, 1947, when Jackie Robinson desegregated the game of baseball, every young prospect in the Dodgers organization felt the impact and grandeur of what was taking place throughout the game. This was a Brigadoon time for baseball. It needed to take that stand, affirming that it was indeed the national pastime—all for one and open to all.

This period right after World War II found America in a positive mood as families were reunited and industry turned from producing war materials to producing automobiles and other durable goods. And baseball's decision to allow Jackie Robinson an equal opportunity was perfectly timed because of the national good mood in America.

The glorification of professional athletes has led to recent back-lashes referring to athletes as "dumb jocks" and management as "corporate sports raiders." However, if it were not for dumb jocks ignoring society's barriers and corporate raiders interested in changing the game, we might not have the social homogenization today that makes the game truly global.

Jackie Robinson was a big-league hero of mine because he was the Rookie of the Year in 1947. To me, he was also a superstar. I was sitting on the fence. I was the hopeful one. In my eyes he had made it—in baseball and in life. I had done neither and was try-ing to climb my way to the majors and have a family that I could come home to.

I was still raw talent—like clothes left on the clothesline to dry off a bit before they're folded and placed with the other fine cloth-ing. Jackie seemed to be the first one to take me off that line—to fold me properly and make me feel as though I belonged with the others.

It was the spring of 1948, an otherwise nondescript day. I had a feeling that this would be an important appearance for me, as I was told shortly before game time that I would be facing the big-league club.

The Dodgers often did that in spring-training games with their top minor-league pitching prospects. They wanted to see arm strength, velocity, stamina. After all, the games are of no signifi-cance in the standings. A win or a loss is as forgotten the next day as what you had for breakfast the day before.

I took the mound that afternoon at LaGrave Field for the Fort Worth Cats wondering how I'd fare against the Dodgers' lineup. They had the stars—Pee Wee, Jackie, Carl Furillo—all playing that day against me. I received no pardon from bench players. "All-stars all the way" was the meal served to me.

I thought I held up well—a little over three innings and noth-ing bad to write home about. I didn't make any mistakes, I didn't groove any fastballs, and I thought I changed speeds well. My curve was working as well, and so I thought my anonymity was a positive.

However, the little voice inside my head still hoped that someone would notice me. Walking off the mound after the fifth inning, I looked around the stands and wondered whether in a few weeks I'd be seeing the same small minor-league ballparks or if instead I'd be at the big cathedral in Brooklyn, preaching to the real choir.

I had been in the minors only a short time, but I had that anticipation running rampant inside my stomach. There were twenty-six farm teams at this time in the Dodgers' system, and there were almost eight hundred good players under Dodgers contracts whom I had to beat out if I wanted that elusive spot on the big-league roster.

After the game was over I smacked the dirt off my cleats, stomping my heels on the old-fashioned dusty dugout floor. I was heading out to the clubhouse, which was located in the outfield and was not accessible from the dugout, when I was summoned back by a teammate's bellow. Someone was there to see me.

This was the era before television, let alone ESPN. Scouting wasn't what we know it as today. This was old-school baseball, and in my era if the organization wanted to hide a top prospect, for whatever the reason, they had the control to accomplish that task. They didn't pigeonhole me, and I was lucky—and I'm extremely grateful to general manager Branch Rickey for that.

"Where's Erskine? Is he in the dugout?" the voice was beckoning.

That voice soon emerged from the thick summer air, and there was the pleasant face to match—a face of friendship, of encouragement, and of grandeur. It imparted grand notions of accomplishment and dreams yet to be fulfilled.

"Hey, young man, I just wanted you to know that I faced you twice today and you won't be long for this league. You're going to be with us real soon!" a straightforward, confident, and honest Jackie Robinson told me in the visitors' dugout.

He said what he had to say, and then he turned and walked away with a smile and a wink.

I was stunned. Words couldn't capture the moment. My mouth was so open my lower lip could have touched the ground.

This was Jackie Robinson, the big leaguer, the Rookie of the Year in 1947, giving me encouragement!

Why me? Why then? Why after the game all alone?

Questions raced through my head but left unanswered, like missed fastballs. Motives and timing didn't matter—it just mattered that I was there and he was talking to me. It wasn't some general pep talk to the guys. It was a special delivery to me.

I was elated, but there was no one to tell. I was left to walk out of the dugout alone, look around at those old wooden stands—painted bright aqua blue with gold and yellow trim—and feel as if it were heaven.

It's every minor-league kid's dream that someone will take note of you, and fortunately for me, *someone* did. And not only was this someone Jackie Robinson, but he related well to the fact that I was a scared minor-league kid, and his action still speaks to me today of the sensitivity and deep character Jackie Robinson possessed. The impact of this gesture resonates mostly from the fact that he didn't *have* to do it.

Much to our modern-day disbelief, Jackie Robinson was not a revered national name back in March of 1948. It seems incongruous to our multicultural minds today that this could be the case, but America in 1947, after two world wars, was still a segregated nation and a nation that accepted that fact—at least as far as our government was concerned.

America, beyond Williamsburg, Brooklyn, labeled Robinson a black man first and a baseball player second. When Mickey Mantle came up, he was touted as this immediate fountain of youth, but America didn't afford Jackie that same pat on the back.

What Jackie accomplished was incredible, but I had come from an area of the country where African Americans lived in my neighborhood. We went to school together. I had a childhood buddy, Johnny Wilson, who was African American, and so to me this was life as usual. Life was about people's souls, not their race or religion or anything else.

2

My First Day at School

THERE *THEY* WERE—JACKIE, Pee Wee, Preacher Roe, and Ralph Branca. My day had finally come, and the hike to Pittsburgh to join up with the team seemed pleasant because I knew that the waiting was over. The worst part of being in the minors is the false encouragement, or the honest encouragement that never materializes into any real job at the big-league level.

The "Sit tight, son," cautioning of Dodgers general manager Branch Rickey was finally over.

As I traveled to Pittsburgh I remembered those minor-league days, particularly how I felt after my stellar nineteen-plus-win season, against only nine losses, in Class B ball. I had also shown the Dodgers organization a terrific winter ball season in Cuba, only to hear the same silence from my phone's ringer. There was a dial tone—the phone worked—but nobody was calling me.

I was beginning to wonder about the Dodgers and whether Rickey's comments were genuine or just lip service.

Leo Durocher, the Dodgers' manager, had applied every type of pressure to Branch Rickey to get me up to the big-league club that spring training, but Rickey had a different outlook.

"He's too green," Rickey kept repeating. He had first told this to Leo when asked about me and the possibility of having me brought up to the big club in early 1948.

"I don't want to ruin him by bringing him up so soon. He hasn't pitched enough. This was only his first full year, plus a winter season in Havana."

And so Branch Rickey got his way, but Leo still protested. When Leo knew he was right, he was in that fight for the full fifteen rounds.

Being in the minor leagues makes a player take stock of himself—where he's come from and where he wants to go—and I often thought about my life in baseball and questioned whether I'd made the right choice. The days of playing catch with my dad were over. The days when he taught me how to throw a curveball by holding a book on how to pitch in one hand and a ball in the other were over. I'll never forget the speech he gave me one day: "Now you hold it like this, bring your arm back, cock your wrist, and rotate it and release it overhand like this . . . !" The next thing I remembered, the ball went flying through the air, bounced through a doorway into the dining room, and broke both the china cabinet door and the dishes and china inside.

"That's one of the best breaks I ever got on a ball," Dad said to me during my mother's hysteria over the broken dishes.

The minors seemed a long way away from that day when he taught me my overhand curve. All I wanted was the opportunity to play in the majors, and I knew I could prove myself. Maybe the Dodgers needed one more piece of proof that I was ready. I decided that I'd bear down in 1948 and really let go, and after a midseason record of fifteen solid wins by mid-July, Branch Rickey finally relented.

The Fort Worth Cats were in Tulsa at the time, and I had just won my fifteenth game. The following morning in the lobby of the Wells Hotel, Burt Shotton approached me. Burt had been a troubleshooter in the Dodgers organization at that time—a sort of roving director of scouting, as he would be termed today.

"Well, son," he started off. "I've just spent forty-five minutes on the telephone convincing Branch Rickey that you're ready and he said OK. So you're going to leave here and join the Dodgers in Pittsburgh."

Victory at last! With my heart racing from anticipation, the trip to the Schenley Hotel in Pittsburgh seemed fast. I checked in as planned and the next morning stood out on the hotel's porch waiting to go to the ballpark. I had planned on arriving at the park extra early because I wanted to get settled in, and standing there I stuck out like a sore thumb with my duffel bag that said "Fort Worth Cats" on it.

I saw the Dodgers' players out on the porch and approached Billy Cox.

"How do you get to Forbes Field?" I asked him. He quickly took note of my duffel bag and put two and two together and retorted, "You take a cab."

Walking briskly downstairs, I hailed a cab.

"Forbes Field, please," I instructed the driver.

"What did you say?" he asked me.

I knew something was wrong when I heard the laughter from the outdoor porch.

"Are these your buddies?" the driver asked me.

"Yes," I mumbled.

"Someone's played a trick on you. Forbes Field is a half a block around the corner. You can walk there in three minutes."

That was my introduction into major-league baseball and major-league clubhouse antics.

I walked around the corner and went inside the ballpark not knowing where to go, was directed to see the visiting clubhouse man, and found my locker, with my little duffel bag still in hand.

My knowledge of Forbes Field was limited. Previously, I knew only about those long home runs Ralph Kiner hit there in Kiner's Korner.

Needless to say, I was a bit timid about the whole situation. Once I was inside the locker room changing into my new uniform, the gray visiting jersey that read "DODGERS" across the chest in blue script, all of my minor-league experiences seemed miles away, another lifetime ago.

Pittsburgh was today. Pittsburgh was the present time.

I also had my first visitor to my locker. Every big leaguer remembers the first guy on the team to come over to his locker and pat him on the back.

"What did I tell you? I told you that you couldn't miss!" Jackie Robinson said with his hand on my shoulder.

Now I felt I belonged. Once again, Jackie had come through for me—and all before we were official teammates.

I was tickled to death to be playing alongside men I admired, but I didn't know any one of them personally yet. I didn't know their idiosyncrasies. I didn't know their political viewpoints. Their families were alien to me. I was just a hungry young man, trying to make my own personal dream of playing big-league ball come true. It was the same dream that took me from Anderson, Indiana, to big-city life in Brooklyn in what seemed like only a few minutes from my new perspective.

I didn't own a car for the longest of whiles, and for the first few months I spent in Brooklyn I lived at the Hanson Place YMCA. I had my corner room, a cot, and a little desk. There was a pay phone in the hallway that cost five cents for a local call. My window overlooked the meat market, and in the early morning I peered out my corner window and saw all of this wholesale meat being sold to local butchers such as Joe Rossi. The men loaded all of this meat up in their trucks, and it was fun to watch. In fact, I was 5–0 living in the YMCA, riding the subway to Ebbets Field, and had three complete games and two wins in relief. I got into a slump after I moved into a house with my wife, Betty, when she joined me in Brooklyn, and I joked to her that I might go back to the YMCA to get myself straightened out.

As for Ebbets Field, its most interesting aspect was the grand rotunda, with its high ceiling and encircled with ticket windows— truly a grand entrance. Architects fascinated by its design would call me inquiring about the blueprints. It was a true neighborhood ballpark, not like some of the parks in other cities.

The other interesting aspect of Ebbets Field, which I later found out was true of many ballparks in the big leagues, was that it faced northeast if you were standing at home plate. The sun was blocked by the outfield stands, making it a dream for the hitter. For the pitcher, however, it was a disadvantage. Late in the afternoon, at about the seventh inning or so, the sun would peek through those I beams from the upper deck and would send a piercing ray of light right into the infielders' eyes. For those minutes when this happened, I was literally throwing blind. The hitter had the advantage, and it was dangerous at times.

Pitcher Billy Loes once complained that he lost a ground ball hit by Vic Raschi in the sun! But he wasn't kidding. The Raschi high hopper bounced in such a way it caught the piercing ray of light and blinded Billy when he reached for the high bounce. The shadows late in the day also played a role in the outcomes of games, and I quickly learned that baseball in the big leagues was a game of inches and of sweat.

"Buy a car, you made it, kid," the guys razzed me my first month up with the big club.

Nothing doing; I knew how fleeting success could be, and I made up my mind that I wasn't having any part of buying a car until I had proved to myself that I'd be in Brooklyn to stay.

The guys meant well, though. They thought that having a car would give me some sense of independence. I wouldn't need to be tied down to the subway schedule. I could have some fun with it.

I mulled it over and slept on it. I made a promise to myself. I'd buy a car if I proved to myself that I was a big leaguer all the way. When I had some big wins under my belt and felt like a major leaguer, and the Dodgers showed me that I was staying in Brooklyn, I went out and bought myself a shiny new car.

I wasn't a car maven or anything, so I asked around. Taking advice from guys like Pee Wee and Duke Snider, I went out and bought myself a 1948 black turtleback two-door Pontiac! This was a big deal to a skinny kid from Indiana.

I practiced driving up and down Ocean Avenue until I got enough nerve to venture out onto the Belt Parkway. Merging with the speeding traffic seemed harder than finding the strike zone in the glaring sun at Ebbets Field.

As for social aspects of the game, Indiana home life prepared me, I felt, for anything. It also left me rather blind to the fact that some people couldn't accept Jackie at first. I didn't understand why. Jackie was a great guy and a great ballplayer. You've heard the expression "dumb ballplayers." I think at times we were all dumb to what was happening outside the game.

Some Dodgers personnel had issues with Jackie at first. They finally realized they were wrong in every respect. But it wasn't a personal problem. Rather, it was a cultural issue with them. Until they shook the childhood ideologies that had been ingrained in them, they were in a sense culturally and socially paralyzed.

A case in point was the Dodgers' announcer Red Barber, who was a sweet, nice man, but who had grown up in the South among folks who had different views on how society ought to be laid out.

And so Red Barber, early on, had a problem with being the announcer on the team when Jackie Robinson was signed. Southern born and bred, he was resistant to change. It wasn't about Jackie as a person but about fear of change. Red talked to his wife about what he should do, and she reminded him of something that at first he was resistant to hearing from her.

"Your duties as a professional broadcaster are to report what is happening on the field and not to be a critic in the booth," she told Red.

Red told me that he was glad his wife was honest with him and that she had straightened him out—but still he remained skeptical as to whether he could do it. However, once he became acquainted with Jackie Robinson, the person, he had the utmost respect for Jackie and became fond of him. He realized that the vacuum he had lived in was wrong on many levels and that it needed to be shaken. He needed to be impartial and understood that it was silly to conceptualize society in distinct categories.

Once anyone, friend or foe, met Jackie Robinson, they liked him instantly and became a supporter. But it was the societal barriers of the times, and the crazy philosophies in people's own heads, that prevented men such as Red Barber from seeing things clearly at first.

"We have to go home and face our friends and our local congressmen and bake-shop owners, carpenters, repairmen, and butchers," was the reason given at the time by some players, coaches, and Southern teammates to explain their resistance toward Jackie at first. Dixie Walker and Bobby Bragan, both from the Deep South, resisted early but changed their opinion once they got to know Jackie.

However, if everyone had adopted that philosophy, baseball would have never changed its ways. Commissioner Happy Chandler might never have encouraged Branch Rickey to allow Robinson to play professional baseball.

August 4, 1948—Jackie stole home in the first inning on Russ Meyers of the Chicago Cubs. Meyers argued vehemently and was thrown out during the brouhaha. His words went out over the radio broadcast, and he was fined. Dutch McCall was brought in to relieve Meyers, and Rex Barney won the game for Brooklyn. But to see a major leaguer steal home—and I had been up in the big leagues for only two weeks—was incredible. Hall of Fame announcer Ernie Harwell remembers the game to this day, because it was the first game he broadcast in the majors. It couldn't get more exciting, or so it seemed then, but it did. Jackie continued to make plays that baffled, amazed, and delighted the fans year in and year out.

And so baseball was more advanced than society and far more accepting and welcoming.

Although it had fisticuffs at times during the 1920s and 1930s and was a sport in which beanballs and bench-jockeying were an integral part, baseball gave this man a chance to be treated as an equal.

By the time I arrived in mid-July of '48 to join the team, Leo had just been acquired as the manager of the accursed Giants. Now I had to stomach him coaching third base in that orange-trimmed uniform with "GIANTS" written across his chest.

And did he ride me! I couldn't believe that this same man who had persuaded Mr. Rickey and scout Clyde Sukeforth that I was really ready was now a sworn enemy the first time he saw me in the big leagues.

Leo must have forgotten all those kind words he had said to Branch Rickey about me, because he complained to the umpires so vociferously about my pitching motion being illegal that I became rattled.

"He's not keeping his foot on the pitching rubber!" Durocher yelled to the home-plate umpire.

"He's rocking back and forth and he's raising his foot up and down. He keeps losing contact with the rubber."

By rule, pitchers must keep in contact with the rubber at all times during the windup, and I knew that I was, but Durocher made me so nervous that I actually balked—and balked in a run at that! Leo was a fiery manager, a maverick who tried anything to win, legal or not, and while he was still my friend, I was now his sworn enemy because he was a Giant.

But that was Leo Durocher. He really rattled my cage that day. One reason why he and Jackie Robinson were alike was that they both knew how to stoke one's fire. This was a great lesson for me early on in my career.

3

How Robinson Rejuvenated Baseball

J ACKIE ROBINSON REJUVENATED BASEBALL much as Babe Ruth had after the 1919 White Sox (Black Sox) scandal. There has been much made about the fact that Ruth's power and his awesome, majestic home runs brought fans to the ballpark. He single-handedly ended the dead-ball era by starting a new era of prodigious slugging and home-run derbies. He also restored honesty, integrity, and child-friendliness to the game of baseball. Ruth brought a dignity to the game that we could all be proud of, and he changed the notion that baseball was filled with hooligans and fist-fighting drunkards. Some of the White Sox had conspired to throw the 1919 World Series, and the whole imbroglio became known as the Black Sox scandal. Commissioner Kenesaw Mountain Landis, a United States district court judge, was brought in to put a stern face on the game and to levy the harshest punishment. "Shoeless" Joe Jackson was kept out of the Hall of Fame. Eight members of the White Sox team were banned for life. Baseball needed a new face, a new idol.

Babe Ruth was that new idol. He was more than a player. Descriptions of him were almost biblical in print coverage. His antics were as grand as his home runs, and his heart was as big as Yankee Stadium. The swelling crowds Ruth drew to the Polo Grounds were the main reason that the Yankees built their own ballpark in the Bronx. But, as with all legends, Ruth's flame eventually died out and a new fire needed to be lit on a new candle.

But not even baseball knew from where to fill Ruth's void. World War II claimed our country's efforts, and superstars such as Joe DiMaggio, Ralph Kiner, Bob Feller, Ted Williams, Hank Greenberg, and Yogi Berra all went off to fight for our freedom.

When World War II ended and these great men returned, they found themselves still side by side with the same African-American men who had also risked life and limb to fight for this glorious nation—theirs as well. The "buffalo soldiers," as they were called, were heroes in every sense of the word. As an officer in the U.S. Army, Jackie Robinson was a hero before he ever stepped on a baseball diamond and before the *New York Times* ever spotlighted his name. Jackie's mother instilled in him a desire to fight for the America he wanted and deserved. Now a war veteran, Robinson returned home to find the same lack of civil rights as when he left. But the game of baseball had other plans for Robinson.

Little did everyone know at the time, but Jackie Robinson was the man who would rejuvenate the game. And by 1949 America embraced Jackie Robinson as its next superstar in sports, let alone baseball, as he graced the covers of magazines and was extended opportunities to appear on national television. However, what the television viewers who were on Jackie's side might not have realized was that when the camera lights were turned off and he left the building to board a bus, he was still treated as a black man first and a man second. And this broke Jackie's heart on a daily basis because he gave his all—body and soul—to the game of baseball.

Jackie brought speed back to the baseball diamond. He brought intensity and honesty in play. Fans came to the ballpark to see Jackie as much as they came to see the ball game. He was exciting to watch, because you never knew if that particular day he'd steal home as he so often did. The art of baserunning and stealing bases had previously been lost to the power-hungry public.

As great an athlete as he was, Robinson's characteristics were unusual. First, he was heavy in the legs and he ran pigeon-toed with a kind of swagger. Lots of players could outrun him in a one-hundred-yard dash. However, it was his quickness that made him a great base runner and base stealer. It took a couple of times around the league for right fielders to understand how to deal with him. When Jackie would get a base hit to right, he would round first base so far that instinctively the right fielder would throw behind him to get him going back to first—and Jackie would be all the way to second by that time. After a while the right fielders just let him make as wide a turn as he wanted around first, and then they'd throw to second. But he had already gotten inside their heads. He had penetrated their psyches and affected their abilities on the field. This was a tremendous shot in the arm for our team.

Another aspect of Jackie that was so interesting was the fact that it was impossible for opponents to catch him in a rundown. His instincts just took over, and he knew how to outsmart everyone. He was so quick that seasoned major leaguers looked like Little Leaguers throwing the ball back and forth trying, however futilely, to catch him in a rundown. He almost invariably caused a bad throw and was called safe by the umpire.

Once, at Ebbets Field, we were playing the Philadelphia Phillies and Jackie was on third base. He got trapped in a rundown play between third and home. Anybody else would have been thrown out, but not Jackie! He caused the infielders to come in and try to help out the catcher and third baseman in the rundown. Soon four players were involved in the rundown between him and home, and then two between him and third base, and Jackie still managed to score! I never saw anything like this in my life. Jackie outwitted them all.

As a hitter, he was par excellence. But his batting style was unique. First, he used a bat with an extremely thick handle and a relatively small barrel. This went against the custom of a thick barrel and thinner handle. The bat was also an ounce or two heavier than the usual thirty-two- to thirty-four-ounce bats used by most players.

Jackie's swing was a "down and through the ball" style. The effect of this style of swing was that when he connected, the downward swing put a tremendous amount of spin on the ball, and this produced vicious line drives. He'd hit shots between the outfielders that were unbelievable. They'd skip off the grass and ricochet off the outfield fences unlike anything that had previously been observed in baseball. Jackie hit home runs, and they were never towering fly balls in full view for the fans to ooh and applaud over. Rather, they were rocket shots. They'd fly off the barrel of the bat so fast that if a player blinked, he often missed it!

As a fielder, Jackie's ability was unparalleled. His fielding was mechanical—no free flow, grace, or acrobatics. He was a workman with a glove. And he was quick. This led to a phenomenal double-play duo in him and Pee Wee. When Pee Wee took the throw from Jackie at second, his relay to first was ballet. When Jackie made the turn it was a freight train coming out of a tunnel. Everybody ducked!

Baseball showcased this man, but society was still dragging its feet. This is why baseball is a game I love: because it affords an equal stage for all who come to play and who love the game. At a time when restaurants in our nation's capital didn't allow Robinson to dine in the regular seating areas, baseball had a locker room shared equally by all.

Baseball has not been properly commended for its insight and its fairness.

Anybody who lived during the post–World War II era knows firsthand that at a time when African Americans could not eat in the same dining rooms, use the same water fountains, and ride in the same Pullman cars as whites in America, baseball decided to do what Washington was reluctant to—take the first step in the civil rights campaign. Baseball was the bright spotlight under which all stars shined equally. When the ball was hit to Jackie Robinson, no one—not his mother, not Mr. Rickey, not his wife, Rachel—could help him. He did it all by himself, and in the process he changed America, the wonderful effects of his bravery still being felt today. It has been said that the journey of a thousand miles starts with the first step—and this was a giant first step.

In order to have both leagues integrated, Mr. Rickey needed a partner in this venture, and he found one in Cleveland Indians owner Bill Veeck, who agreed to sign the power-hitting African-American outfielder Larry Doby. Together, Branch Rickey and Bill Veeck helped further the America we know today more so than any congressman or senator in the years directly following World War II.

Jackie was nearly court-martialed because of an incident that took place on a bus while he was in the service. Even our own military considered Robinson an African American first and a soldier second, though he was risking his life to fight for his country.

Jackie had strong resolve, strong religious conviction instilled in him by his mother, and a strong wife behind him, and so he was able to persevere, as was Larry Doby, who made his debut just weeks after Jackie's own.

At the time, in 1947, Branch Rickey had a list of fifty candidates and selected Jackie Robinson based on a strong recommendation from Clyde Sukeforth. Larry Doby was second on that list, and Branch Rickey and Bill Veeck agreed to force the issue and make society, if just in the realm of baseball, change. Those two men forced a social issue that had scared many a politician. If it had been up to Congress to integrate baseball, Jackie and I often wondered how long it would have taken for that change to occur.

There was a ho-hum attitude around the country as to what was taking place in baseball in the spring of '47, with few players adamantly against Jackie, even fewer adamantly for him, and the majority in a neutral position. But this wasn't a situation where another country remained neutral while we fought against Europe. America won that World War. This war—the war going on in the city streets to determine a man's right to have the same opportunity as any other man—was taking place on our soil.

The game rested in the hands of the writers, who acted as the liaisons to the fans because there wasn't any television sports media as we know it today. The writers approached this opportunity with an interesting outlook—they were waiting to see how the baseball side of Jackie would fare. The answer was an immediate and resounding "yes," that Jackie was indeed as great as the legend behind his feats at UCLA. By taking solid control of the chance that baseball afforded him, Jackie, and then Larry Doby, allowed sports to view society differently than ever before, and in turn changed the way men viewed other men. But as a country we still had a long way to go, and the point was immediately ingrained in my mind in 1948 when I saw what went on in the various big-league cities. But in 1949 an incident happened that nobody could have predicted.

In 1949, on the heels of the Korean War, an African-American person could not enter a restaurant through the same entrance as a white Southerner in the Deep South. This was not only accepted, but if you were to walk up to someone on the street and ask him why this was the case, he'd look at you as if you were nuts for asking. It was an all-too-comfortable way of life for much of America at the time.

One fateful day back in 1949 at Ponce de Leon Park in Atlanta, Georgia, we arrived to find the KKK picketing and death threats to Jackie. And this was merely an exhibition game.

Jackie's sister, Willa Mae, was scared that he was going to be shot. We were all scared and took the threats very seriously. While we as athletes always took fans to be rather harmless and more exuberant than anything, this was different. It wasn't some heckler, a harmless nutcase in the bleachers, or an angry die-hard base-ball fan of another team. This was a real-life death threat.

Burt Shotton read the letter aloud in the clubhouse: "Take the field and you're going to be shot!"

If ever a clubhouse of strapping young men was at a loss for words, this was the time. I never in my life saw a clubhouse that numb and that dumbfounded. We were lost. We couldn't believe anybody would want to kill somebody else for playing ball because of his race.

The atmosphere was so tense that something was needed in the way of comic relief. Outfielder Gene Hermanski came to the res-cue in the same fashion he had once done to umpire Jocko Con-lan. Jocko had missed a call for our club and later needed a ride to another game in spring training, and so we offered him our plane to ride with us. Jocko was all prepared for the ride when sud-denly, over the PA system, instead of the captain speaking, it was Gene: "Jocko! Jocko! This is your conscience speaking! Give up!"

This time around, Gene once again came to the aid of the mor-bid locker room to relax us all, including Jackie. Jackie had already made up his mind to take the field; but an eerie feeling of uncer-tainty permeated the clubhouse.

"Why don't we all wear number 42? Then the nut won't know who to shoot at?" Gene Hermanski said with aplomb.

Jackie thought that was the topper of them all. But that was Gene. He didn't have a bad bone in his body, only funny ones. He was another guy who helped Jackie feel at home in the majors. Jackie was the fabric of the Brooklyn Dodgers. He was our team-mate, our friend, and our ally. We only prayed he felt likewise about us.

Pugnacious and always controversial Dick Young, a legendary writer for the *New York Daily News*, stirred the pot even more that hot day in Atlanta by gaining an exclusive with Dr. Green, who was the leader of the KKK and a medical doctor to make matters worse.

Young asked Green if he'd prescribe medicine to an African-American patient who needed it—and stopped the man in his tracks. After all, he had taken the Hippocratic oath, which was blind to race, religion, and nationality.

But not even Dick Young knew what lay ahead—a ballpark without one African-American fan as far as the eye could see. The Klan picketed the park. Crowds swelled inside and out.

And then Jackie protested along with pitcher Don Newcombe and catcher Roy Campanella, and finally the black fans were permitted to sit on a levee behind the right-field fence, because they weren't allowed to buy tickets. To see a stadium segregated like that was just another sign that we as a country were two societies —the baseball society and the outside world of real-life society— and it was up to twenty-five men wearing a different type of uniform to change the way America viewed itself and the way Americans viewed one another.

"Jackie, do you mind moving over a few feet to your right?" a laughing Pee Wee asked during on-field warm-ups. "This guy might be a bad shot." Jackie laughed. Pee Wee's needle had two points: one, it was a good-natured jab; two, it was another way of saying, "You're one of us."

Baseball was the only medium where no matter where we traveled, the locker room was an equal room. There were twenty-five lockers without distinction. Men dressed next to one another and played on the same diamond with one another. Baseball was more socially advanced than our own society at the time, and the game deserves a heck of a lot of credit for standing up and taking the first step when every other facet of society refused to.

Jackie Robinson broke barriers not only on the field but off it as well. His on-the-field performance was rivaled by no other Dodgers player, and his off-the-field civic endeavors were also second to none. He firmly believed in self-help, the same philosophy that guides his foundation, which his wife, Rachel, heads today: *Get prepared. Be ready. Deliver.*

Jackie needed to quell his anger the first couple of years, a task that only someone with his inner strength and vision could have accomplished at that moment. When I reflect and wonder what it must have been like for a man who should have been at the happiest moments in his life to still have to deal with racial indignities on a daily basis, it is mind-boggling. Most men would have cracked.

Jackie couldn't even purchase a home in most areas of Connecticut. His saving grace was that he found a sleepy town — Stamford. Jackie and Rachel purchased a house there and decided that this would be where they would start their family.

At a time when mortgage lenders and real estate agents were helping Jim Crow stand, baseball was trying to knock Jim Crow on its back. There was a backlash by prospective neighbors when Jackie was trying to buy a house. So deals fell through like lazy fly balls in the shadows. We were a society blinded by ourselves, but baseball wasn't blinded.

Baseball allowed Jackie to see if he could stand up to the pressures outside the white lines and realize his dreams, and Jackie was always thankful to the game, and his genuine thankfulness made him a great ambassador for the game.

Branch Rickey and the Dodgers organization gave Jackie Robinson that opportunity, and Jackie was grateful, as was Rachel. Happy Chandler, the commissioner of baseball at the time, was supportive of Rickey's experiment and lobbied the other owners to permit Jackie to enter the league. Some owners felt it would hurt attendance. Were they ever wrong! Mr. Rickey, a master communicator, sold Chandler on the idea, and although Commissioner Landis had been more resistant, I think Rickey could have sold Landis or anybody else because he too was on a mission and was not going to let anyone stand in his way.

Many Hall of Fame ballplayers have left marks on the game, but few can honestly be labeled "game changers." And Don Newcombe was living proof, as were Joe Black and Roy Campanella, of how Jackie Robinson made the players around him better. They observed how Jackie played the game and adapted their game accordingly.

One particular afternoon in 1949 found rookie pitcher Don Newcombe in a predicament. Don was a burly, hard-throwing right-hander. He had an 11–1 lead early on in the fourth inning in a game at Pittsburgh's Forbes Field, where I had made my major-league debut the year before, and was having trouble throwing strikes. He started aiming the ball, and that made matters worse. Jackie came to the mound to bolster Newk's confidence.

"Why don't you just go on in and shower? You don't act like you want to win this one. See that bullpen out there? There are three guys who hope you leave—they want this easy win," Jackie told Don.

"Go on inside and shower, or reach back and throw the damn ball!" Robinson finished his soliloquy.

Newk looked at him, said nothing, and proceeded to finish strong. And he of course got the win. Jackie always knew that getting inside Newk's head like that and rattling his cage a bit made him pitch better. And he used this same technique on several occasions with Don over the course of his career. But Campy was the opposite.

Jackie would come out to the mound as if to confer with Newk on other occasions and give him a blast or two, challenging his character. Newk would stand there and take it. Campanella would then jog to the mound and soothe Don in his own way: "It's just you and me, Roomie. You've got all it takes. You're going to win this one." Cool and easy, Campy soothed Newk every time and emotionally stroked his confidence, like a balm on a wound.

But Newk needed Jackie's remarks just as much to stoke his fire.

Every time this happened, Newk took his game to a new level. He'd blow away hitter after hitter and usually retire the side inning by inning until he finished the job. I'd be in the middle, amused by it all. It was a tale of two different men and two different approaches to baseball and life—and two men who loved and respected each other.

Campanella had a "let it be" attitude, and it worked for him. He wanted to focus only on the positive and wanted no part of any problems or complaints. He was in his own world, and I understood him. Roy was a decent, wonderful family man who admired Jackie, and Jackie admired Roy's rise to the majors and all he had overcome in his life. Both men truly respected one another.

Jackie made Newk a better pitcher that day, just as he made his teammates better players, better teammates, and more aware of what was happening in our society.

Babe Ruth had been that type of player for the Yankees—and made Lou Gehrig and Tony Lazzeri and the players around him better. His home-run power, off-the-field generosity, and grandness of character that went beyond the game made Ruth a legend. But when the legend retired, we needed that void filled. Jackie was the man to fill it.

Jackie Robinson, with his unparalleled speed on the base paths and the electricity he brought with him every time he reached base and took a stride, brought fans first to the stands and then to their feet. His 1949 National League MVP Award, for which he edged out Stan "the Man" Musial, was proof that the sportswriters were not going to refute his incredible impact on the game. Jackie's election to the National Baseball Hall of Fame in 1962 on his first ballot of eligibility is further proof of that impact.

And when Jackie was elected to the Hall of Fame, he used that status to further civil rights because this honor represented, to him, the fact that one society—the baseball society—respected him on an equal basis. And if baseball could respect him as an equal, then he felt America should afford all African Americans that same respect.

4
The Story of Rachel

RACHEL ROBINSON PLAYED A HUGE role in Jackie's triumph over racism because she gave him a much-needed release from his on-field and off-field distractions. All major leaguers get verbally taunted by opposing teams; the visiting clubs view it as a baseball rite of passage. However, in Jackie's case, he often reflected to me on this phenomenon by questioning where the line was where the bench-jockeying stopped and racism in the heart began.

I felt as clueless as anyone because I was not from an environment where there was racial taunting, and I also couldn't get any better glimpse into a man's heart than anyone else could.

Sometimes, as in Philadelphia, the answer was clear. Sometimes it wasn't so clear, and it drove the fire in Jackie's belly.

Rachel told my wife, Betty, that Jackie would come home from the ballpark and just go outside and pound golf balls as a release. This was his anger management. He channeled his energy into golf and through civil duties he felt he needed to support.

Although Jackie stood alone on the field—as when he'd have to cover second base and ready himself for a hard, spikes-up slide by the base runner trying to break up the double play—Rachel was his Rock of Gibraltar off the field.

She once told me that Jackie was as quiet and gentle at home as he was tenacious on the field. It didn't seem odd to her because after all she had married a man who had proved to be a loyal, faithful boyfriend and a decent standout citizen at UCLA.

Jackie needed Rachel, and that's one of the reasons why Mr. Rickey was convinced Robinson was the right man to make change happen.

Mr. Rickey had this quiz he liked to give all prospective players who were about to ink their first big-league contract at his Montague Street office. The questions centered around social life and whether the player had a girlfriend, had hobbies, attended religious services, and what he did after supper.

Mr. Rickey wanted to know *who* he was inviting onto his team. He wanted to know the person of Jackie Robinson. He knew the athlete Jackie Robinson because Clyde Sukeforth attested to Jackie's ability, as did Chicago manager Jimmy Dykes, who, after seeing Robinson play, proclaimed, "Jackie Robinson could play in the big leagues on a moment's notice."

So Rickey knew the ballplayer. He wanted to know the man. He knew that John Roosevelt Robinson was born on January 31, 1919, in Cairo, Georgia, and that he was a four-sport letterman standout at UCLA. The stats were a given. Rickey now desired to go on an emotional and spiritual journey, one that tested his own fortitude if he could make this happen, and so he delved into the forces behind the man.

Rickey liked what he saw. He saw a man raised by a Christian mother, Mallie Robinson. He saw a good man who was kind to his sister, Willa Mae Robinson, and respected his brothers. And he saw a man who had a fantastic wife in Rachel Robinson. He saw a man devoted to his God and to the ideals set forth in the Bible.

Rickey was convinced about Jackie. The hardest task lay in a request he made of Jackie—a request that would have tested the mettle of any man and that would have been failed by all but a man of Robinson's inner strength. This was the idea of not striking back, of turning the other cheek to the abuse he was sure to receive.

Rickey was convinced that if Jackie was shown how important this step was for all the other players in the Negro Leagues, he would be able to refrain from striking back for three years.

Jackie agreed with Mr. Rickey. The "gag rule" would be in full force for three years, and then Jackie would be free to do whatever he wanted. Once again, true freedom had its initial strings. This was a man who as a kid went swimming in a reservoir and ended up being interrogated behind bright lights used for adult criminals by a local sheriff who sent out for watermelon and proceeded to humiliate Jackie and his friends. This was a man who had fought for his wonderful country, as he often referred to the United States, and was nearly court-martialed for failing to sit at the back of a bus. When I was interviewed for Mark Reese's tribute to the Brooklyn Dodgers and I saw the final screening of the movie, I was as shocked hearing about these incidents once again as I had been when Jackie first told me about them.

In the beginning it was a three-year gag rule, but after the second year, 1948, Mr. Rickey released Jackie from year three. Jackie's feelings were so pent-up that they gushed out, and he began to challenge almost anything that had a hint of racism. Mr. Rickey once said he maybe should have held Jackie to the original three-year agreement, but I think Jackie would still have been outspoken.

Rachel is a story in herself because she stood by Jackie, as the Good Book says, tempered his fire, and affected his life in a positive manner. The first couple of years in Brooklyn, Jackie told me, took their toll on him, but not on her. She held back the tears—for his sake—and the angst so that they could persevere together. She made Jackie a calmer person and in so doing made him a better player. I don't think he would have lasted without her by his side.

You see, when the game was over, he always had Rachel to confide in and to air his problems to—problems that he might not always have been able to air in public.

When Jackie was six months old, his dad took off and left the family. Mallie now had to raise five children all by herself. She left sharecropping because she couldn't renegotiate a contract with the farmer, and she decided to take the kids west to Pasadena, California. She purchased a house at 121 Pepper Street. A fighter, Mallie was determined to make it, and hence Jackie learned at an early age that in Jim Crow America, anything that's worthy is worth fighting for.

Jackie showed his mom the pride he had in his family and upbringing by becoming the first four-sport letterman in UCLA history—baseball, basketball, football, and track. And Rachel stood by his side every step of the way.

When Jackie headed off to serve in World War II, it was Rachel in whom he confided about the ignominious treatment he received at Camp Hood. When he came home from the war and headed to Kansas City to play in the Negro Leagues for the Monarchs, there was Rachel. And when a brash Branch Rickey in 1947 decided it was time to bring Jackie up from the minors, Rachel headed to Brooklyn with Jackie—in the back of the bus. When she cried, it was mostly in private. She didn't want Jackie to fight battles for her that would have destroyed his campaign in baseball, and in society.

If there is one moral to the story of Rachel Robinson, it is that a man is more of a man when he has a good woman by his side. Branch Rickey was right—once again. After he met Rachel, he knew immediately that Jackie would succeed.

I knew Babe Ruth's wife. She was constantly answering questions about the Babe and was never able to be herself. Rachel, while responding to the endless questions about her life with Jackie, has been—through philanthropy—her own woman. She was Jackie's greatest support but also his toughest critic.

5

Bedlam in Manhattan, Doom in Brooklyn—1951

AMERICANS REMEMBER WHERE they were the day John F. Kennedy was assassinated. It was a shocking moment in our culture to have a president killed in office. We mourned. We grieved. We felt the pain and felt for our country.

Baseball is a pastime of ours, but it remains only a sport. It's not life and death. However, within the history of the game there are moments when fans feel such a part of the situation that they similarly remember what they were doing and where they were when certain events occurred. I was involved in one such moment—with my team on the wrong end of baseball immortality.

Brooklyn Dodgers fans remember where they were, what they were doing, and what they felt like that fateful day in October of 1951, when the Giants beat us to win the National League pennant and go on to play the Yankees in the 1951 World Series.

"The Giants win the pennant! The Giants win the pennant!!" an out-of-his-mind Russ Hodges screamed over the radio airwaves from what seemed like Manhattan to the shores of California. But win they indeed did. A walk-off home run, baseball immortality, television shows, instant international fame—all awaited young Bobby Thomson.

The demographics of the Giants were interesting. They played in Upper Manhattan and their fans acted like elitists, as if the only team worth rooting for was their Giants. It was a clear and obvious choice to them. True to their fighting spirit, they were managed by the no-holds-barred mentality of their feisty pugilist manager, Leo Durocher. The same man who had rallied for my arrival to the majors was now at the helm of the rival Giants, and he took no prisoners.

The Giants' fans were typically hard-nosed and loyal. They loved a good fight—looked for it on more than one occasion—and when you add to that the fact that both the Dodgers and the Giants were in the National League, it didn't take a mathematician long to figure out that with each league having just eight teams, the Dodgers and Giants played each other twenty-two times a season—eleven home games and eleven on the road.

All in the same city!

There is the age-old classic story of a rabid Giants fan calling Duke Snider "Horseface." Any edge they could get they took. Only this fan followed Duke to all of the games at the Polo Grounds.

Making fun of the Brooklynese accent, getting personal with the backgrounds of our players, making our lives coming out of that Polo Grounds clubhouse miserable—they did it all with aplomb.

We felt we needed some sort of team vindication, as we had already lost to the Yankees in the 1949 World Series, a series that lasted only five games. But it was not lost without a hard fight.

The Yankees won the first game 1–0, and we won the second game by the same score. They eked out a third-game victory in the top of the ninth for a final score of 4–3—we scored two at the end of the ninth but fell short of tying the game. We lost the third game to them by a 6–4 score, and we lost Game 5 10–6. But we were rookies in that World Series. They were the old pros. This was the Joe DiMaggio series, the Tommy Henrich series, the Phil Rizzuto series.

These guys knew how to win. They were the Bombers, after all. So for our first trip to the dance, we tangoed pretty well and came home with high hopes and no broken toes.

Unfortunately, we came up short in the end, but each game was close, and nobody was more proud of our valiant efforts than Jackie. He had won the National League MVP that season and felt the time was ripe for a championship ring. Although this was not to be, we kept ourselves in the game, and when we lost that fifth and deciding game we knew that we'd come back strong in 1950.

But in 1950 we lost the pennant to the Phillies' "Whiz Kids" team in a backbreaking loss on the final day of the season. Any other team would have been sent to the showers for a few years, but not us. Still, another event in 1950 gave me an unusual glimpse at how Jackie was processing his experiences as a Dodger. It happened on an otherwise nondescript day at Ebbets Field.

I swear I felt as startled, even as embarrassed, as I had ever felt in the big leagues this particular day, and for reasons that were unrelated to baseball.

We had just finished a game at Ebbets Field early in the season. I walked outside the ballpark where the players' families gathered, and — in front of the gathered fans — I kidded around with Jackie Jr., Jackie's son, and Rachel. As advanced socially as baseball was at the time, America was still far behind, but for the most part Brooklyn was as liberal as baseball was in its tolerance and multicultural attitudes.

"I want to thank you, Carl, for what you did out there in front of all those fans yesterday," Jackie said in his serious, unmistakable voice next time I saw him in the clubhouse.

"Jackie, you can thank me for a well-pitched game, but don't ever thank me for what just came naturally," I said with a smile, and Jackie knew I meant it. He was beginning to see that all whites were not opponents.

It was chilling to hear a man thank me for just having a normal conversation. It really made me reflect on what he was going through in his life. I was an average kid from Anderson, Indiana. That incident made me immediately think about myself and my own values instilled in me by my parents. I thought of the fields of Indiana, the heartland, and the friends I made along the way.

Johnny Wilson was a childhood buddy of mine. He and I had played together since grammar school. He and his three brothers and a sister were raised by a single mother. The family was dirt poor but held themselves in high esteem. He went on to lead his high school basketball team in Indiana to its state championship in 1946—and he was named Mr. Basketball in Indiana. When I went on to play minor-league baseball in the Dodgers organization, Johnny played for the Chicago American Giants in the Negro Leagues and later played professional basketball for the famous Harlem Globetrotters! To this day, we often reflect on those precious years of our youth, our days in the sunshine, when we're together.

We both agree that the years flew by; one day we were in uniforms in baseball and were sixteen years old, and the next day we're in our seventies. No more Shadeland Elementary School. No more school basketball team practices. We won the 1938–39 city championship together and played summer baseball together on the American Legion team, and now that seems a lifetime ago. In high school we were starters on the 1944 Anderson Indians, rated number one in the state that year, and only the memories and the newspaper clippings remain.

Johnny knew that good advice didn't come around too often, and so he listened to that good advice when it did come, and he earned his degree in education. After his playing days were over he went on to teach and coach high school and junior college. It was Johnny who taught me to be color-blind, and it was Jackie who taught me to be "better," not bitter, whenever adversity struck.

The incident when Jackie thanked me for talking to his family forever etched itself into my psyche because it documents the struggles this man had trying to do the thing he loved—play baseball. And through all of this he was a leader. He led us to the 1949 World Series, and he led us to challenge the Whiz Kids in 1950, and we knew he'd lead us to the pennant in 1951.

During spring training in 1951 there was a sense of bitterness in the air about how we let the Phillies take the pennant from us. We wanted to decisively win the pennant in '51 and make it our year to howl. We had a new skipper at the helm in Charlie Dressen. Our owner, Walter O'Malley, had gotten rid of many from the Rickey generation, but not Buzzy Bavasi, the team's general manager, because Buzzy knew the organization too well to be fired. If Buzzy had been axed, then Walter would have had to find someone who knew the entire farm system and who knew the scouting reports like Buzzy did.

While playing the Giants that summer, a few of our players were riding Leo about his wife, actress Larraine Day, and Jackie laughed about the fact that Leo got so riled up he actually started making his way toward the Dodgers' dugout from the third-base coach's box and had to be coaxed back to the box.

This was all within the limits of good sportsmanship, or good rivalry, but a curious event happened that went beyond those limits, and it tested the mettle of our team—a test we failed in the end.

Fate has a strange way of biting you in the back if you tempt it. Maybe *some* of the Dodgers should have waited to howl.

The Giants got off to a slow start that season and had lost eight straight. We swept a three-game series at Ebbets Field, extending their streak to eleven. Dressen was paranoid about beating Leo, a feeling that stemmed from his days as Leo's bench coach in Brooklyn. Leo was always good copy for the press and garnered all the accolades; Dressen was a smart baseball man who actually had made many of the decisions. Beating Leo had become the most important thing in his life. Now he had Leo down, and he wanted to kick him. Charlie came down our row of lockers and enlisted all the players to go to the door that separated the two clubhouses and made it convenient for players from opposing teams to visit with each other before games, and sing "Roll Out the Barrel. The Giants are dead! The Giants are dead!" Hermanski refused. Barney and Palika refused. Jackie and Roy vehemently refused. I vehemently refused. Clem Labine refused. But some didn't, and they sang that song loudly through the door. This infuriated Leo so much he complained to Warren Giles, the National League president. Giles ordered that the door be bricked shut, and so it was—and so it remained until the wrecking ball finally destroyed Ebbets Field, long after both teams headed West.

Maybe Durocher and Dressen gave Humphrey Bogart the inspiration for *The Caine Mutiny*, released first in 1954, because they were both paranoid men straight out of the movie.

Charlie Dressen and Leo Durocher were much alike in managerial philosophy. Both were former big-league infielders. Both came from the old school of managing—and both were gamblers.

They ran the team. They were in charge. You knew that loud and clear from the moment you dusted off your cleats in the locker room, and if a rookie didn't know it, he'd learn that lesson mighty quickly.

Their philosophy was, "If your arm hurts, it must be in your head."

Neither of these men had ever pitched in the big leagues; nevertheless, this was the mantra of the day with most managers, and the managers were completely in charge. And Dressen thought he understood pitching, as did most managers who never were pitchers. These were the days before the pitching coach was a former pitcher who truly understood all the aspects of pitching.

The old-time managers' pithy advice on the mound was, "Don't give this guy anything good to hit—but don't walk him!"

Leo Durocher was more demonstrative than Dressen, more military style. It has been poetically phrased that Leo could get a player to want "to run through a brick wall," as my teammate Clyde King used to say.

Dressen had his soft moments, even though he was tough as nails. Whenever we lost two in a row, the locker room had a serious tone to it—a sense of an imperative win, never to allow the opposition a sweep of a miniseries. We had lost two in a row and Charlie laced into us. We then lost three in a row, and he tried the soft approach. We lost four in a row and then he got John Griffin, our clubhouse manager, to "get out the good stuff." He broke out the vodka, bourbon, scotch, and Charlie's favorite—Harveys Bristol Cream.

"This is not for you," Charlie told me. "You're driving your buddies home to Bay Ridge."

And then Charlie added, "And you're pitching tomorrow."

Within an hour our team got real loose and really loud. When the party was finally over at about one-thirty, I let Preacher Roe out at his house; his singing was so loud he must have woken up the whole neighborhood. He couldn't understand how his wife, Mozee, had heard him come in because, after all, he had taken his shoes off! The next day we beat the Phillies 5–1.

I will say that Dressen and Durocher both had effects on their teams that were much more positive than negative.

Jackie, likewise, had that similar effect on me—the need to be prepared but also to let loose at times. His intensity in the dugout and on the field lit a fire in me for some reason, and his raucous sense of humor encouraged me.

Jackie also must have taken a page from Leo's book on how to intimidate the opposition. He was a master at psychological warfare. Newk learned the art of verbal banter well from Jackie, and the two gave it to Leo during the season.

But Leo was alone at the top in his paranoia.

He was the manager of managers. Leo heard baseball voices all the time. And as in *The Caine Mutiny*, the true captain-of-the-ship mentality inside of him brought out the ballistic side of his personality. At this point in the season, Leo was whipped; however, he never gave up. He firmly believed the Giants would pull dead even with us and overtake us in the end to win the pennant! Naturally, he kept motivating the Giants—but how could he hope to overcome a 13½-game lead as late in the season as August?

Leo the Lip and the Giants were ready to wade out in deep waters this season. They were determined to make this one *theirs*.

Slowly, the gap began to shrink.

And so the questions started spewing in our direction. Why did our guys let the Giants back in the pennant race? What was responsible—bad pitching or lack of hitting?

The columnists battled each other. *The Daily Mirror, New York Herald-Tribune, New York Daily News*, and *Brooklyn Eagle* all ran competing stories. Writers vied for the best scoop of the day, the newest wrinkle, anything they could get their hands on. Suddenly the Yankees were back-page news to the NL pennant race. We read the papers. The Giants read the papers. We never lost confidence, but the Giants were putting together an exceptional finish.

The chatter on the street was baseball—and which team was better. This was a dialogue that quickly escalated into other categories.

Which was better? Central Park or Prospect Park? Coney Island or Jones Beach? Brooklyn or Manhattan? A true "Battle of the Boroughs" took place that year, and in the end the winner of a three-game National League playoff would be headed to the Bronx, to face the big, bad Yankees in the 1951 World Series.

It was an all–New York affair, and not a single family was immune from the game of baseball that September.

During the summer of 1951 we made a four-for-four trade with the Chicago Cubs to acquire Andy Pafko. A solid outfielder and hitter, he was to help us quite a bit down the stretch.

Our lineup was making great defensive plays, especially Billy Cox, our third baseman, who was a terrific fielder, "a human octopus"—before Tommy Lasorda used the expression to describe the Yankees' Graig Nettles in the 1978 World Series. Billy had quick, soft hands, and he used a tiny three-fingered glove. The last two fingers, usually separated in most gloves, were one big finger in Billy's. He said he liked this because it afforded him more control. I had never seen anyone use that kind of glove before in the major leagues, and he made some unreal stops at the hot corner with that mitt.

Newk had a phenomenal year in 1951, going 20–9—a .690 winning percentage. He was young, strong, and durable, the kind of starting pitcher who keeps his team from having a long losing streak.

October of 1951 was the month when it all broke loose—all the animosity, the tension, the hard feelings, the rivalry, the Polo Grounds–Ebbets Field mayhem.

Jackie and Newk really had *professional* hatred for Leo Durocher. It didn't venture beyond baseball, and it was symbolic of the rivalry between Giants and Dodgers fans.

The other side to Jackie Robinson that many didn't get to see, but which I sat near enough to observe, was his ability to do the best bench-jockeying of anybody in the majors. He seared Durocher with some of his biting remarks. It was a form of eloquent professional hatred rolled up into a ball of biting irreverent humor that would have made anyone laugh at the mere shock of hearing the comments.

Leo was a dashing dresser. He was the "debonair manager," and his marriage to Larraine Day gave him a true Hollywood connection. And Leo could dish it out. But Jackie could take it and dish it right back with a couple more scoops of verbal abuse.

"They had to change the rules to get you in here!" Leo shouted to Newk.

"Go see what time it is on Babe Ruth's watch!" Newk shouted back to Leo.

This stopped Leo in his tracks.

There had been a rumor concerning Babe Ruth when Leo was a fancy-fielding Yankees shortstop. Babe Ruth had been given a watch as an award. It suddenly disappeared from his locker. No one knew who stole it, but there was a rumor that Leo had it. It was unproved but was always surfacing as an answer to Leo's biting and personal remarks. But that was Jackie and his disciple, Don Newcombe. Jackie taught Newk the art of winning and the art of verbal sparring. After all, Jackie was as intent on winning a game of hearts on the train rides across the country as he was about getting a good lead off first base. The Giants just pumped him up even more so.

I'll never forget that gloomy October sky in fall's start of 1951. We won't pen the date because it's too painful.

The Giants had managed over the course of the summer to pull even with us at the season's end, eclipsing the thirteen and a half–game lead we had built up by the All-Star break.

The season ended dead even, and Jackie kept us alive on the final day by beating the Pirates with a homer in the fourteenth inning. Now a three-game playoff was upon us. The winners went to 161st and River Avenue to face the Yanks, and the losers headed home for an off-season of answering why they lost.

It figures that it was the beginning of October, Halloween month, when the orange colors of the Giants howled the loudest.

There were three of us in the bullpen at the Polo Grounds that fateful October day—me, Ralph Branca, and Clem Labine—plus pitching coach Clyde Sukeforth and two bullpen catchers.

In the bottom of the ninth, with the Dodgers leading 4–2, the call was made to the bullpen. Branca and I were throwing and were both ready. It seemed that in the blink of an eye Dressen was already out of the dugout.

"Who's got the best stuff?" was the question of the day from the dugout to the bullpen. "They're both OK," said Sukey, "but Erskine is bouncing his overhand curve at times." It just went to show how little former catchers know about being pitching coaches. They make great managers for strategy reasons, but without proper pitching coaches, it's hard to judge how a pitcher really looks.

A good pitching coach knows what the pitcher does and can tell the manager, "His fastball is too straight. There's no movement. His curve is lazy." It's difficult, however, for a coach to know the emotional side of things, the stress and fatigue factors that are involved.

It wasn't until the mid-1950s that you started seeing actual former pitchers as pitching coaches, and the Yankees had one of the best in Jim Turner. He was the one who converted Bob Turley and Don Larsen, a couple of young hard throwers who were wild, into solid pitchers. Jim invented the no-windup delivery. It was a hands-in-front-of-the-belt, lock, and pitch motion without a pumping motion. He was about the first specialist in baseball when it came to pitching. And this helped New York because a high percentage of games are won or lost on the mound.

It took baseball almost a hundred years to begin using former pitchers as pitching-coach specialists; up to that point, most pitching coaches had been catchers. I once complained of soreness in my shoulder, even though I was 5–0 at the time, to interim manager Burt Shotton. He looked at me rather surprised and said,

"Well, son, for a kink in your arm go out to the center-field flag-pole and throw straight up the flagpole. That'll get the kink out." He was a former outfielder and didn't understand pitching. Dressen didn't understand pitching, either. It wasn't that he choked or overused pitchers as much as that he wasn't informed because of the way the game was structured back then.

Charlie Dressen went to the mound and made the gesture for Ralph Branca to come into the game and relieve Don Newcombe, who had been baffling Giants all day and throwing hard right until the bitter end. Don told Dressen that he felt he was throwing the ball well and could be effective, and he wasn't all that fond of leaving the game. Don never wanted to be taken out of any game. He had a competitive edge to him, and that's what made him a great pitcher—a Cy Young Award winner—instead of merely a good pitcher. Newk had pitched numerous times down the stretch that season with only two days' rest. He was tired, but his heart was still pumping Dodger blue.

Tenacity—as Robinson taught me—separates those that rise to the occasion once and those that rise daily, and eventually to stardom.

But Dressen's mind was made up. Ralph Branca entered the game, trotting in from the bullpen and wearing his traditional number 13, which didn't seem foreboding at the time.

And on his second pitch—a fastball up and in, the Giants' Bobby Thomson, with Willie Mays on deck, hit a sinking line drive some 315 feet into the lower deck—a three-run home run to win the game and pennant for the Giants. I think if they would have resurrected Cy Young, even he'd have thrown the pitch. Fate was determined that Bobby would hit the walk-off homer to win it for the "Jints."

This was a devastating loss for us, and the most devastating part was the reliving of it in the newsreels and Russ Hodges's call: "The Giants win the pennant! The Giants win the pennant!"

The bullpen crew was the first to arrive at the center-field club-house—the television crews were hurrying to move the cameras from the side of the Dodgers, who they thought would wrap up the game easily, to the Giants' side. Only one door separated the two clubhouses—something not done in today's game.

The cases of champagne were suddenly being hurried from our side to the Giants' locker room. Our clubhouse was dead silent while outside the entire ballpark was in a state of bedlam.

I was one of the first ones who had arrived inside the clubhouse, and I saw with my own eyes the shuffling around of champagne and TV cameras from our clubhouse to theirs.

And then the room was no longer empty.

One by one, my Dodgers teammates, after leaving the field and dugout, came trudging up the narrow stairs to our clubhouse.

From the stool in front of my locker I watched, trying not to stare, as each somber, dejected Dodger came through that club-house door. I wanted to notice their behavior. I did have a sense of history being made and wanted to see the drama unfold.

Gil Hodges strode to his locker, folded his big first baseman's mitt, and placed it gently on the top shelf. For a big, burly man, he was sheepishly quiet.

Jackie stomped to his locker and slammed his rolled-up infielder's glove hard into the back of his metal locker, making a huge "boom."

Manager Charlie Dressen stood by his locker for a brief period, and then he suddenly ripped his uniform down the front, popping off every button.

Ralph Branca, cap off, flopped himself on the eight or ten steps leading up to the trainer's room. I had fought superstition my whole career, trying not to get into that trap. However, I've wondered whether Ralph tempted fate too far when he picked uni-form number 13. He later left with his then fiancée, Ann, and went to dinner privately.

We all dressed in complete silence. Almost in unison, we exited and went out to face our Brooklyn fans. Believe me, that was tougher than the loss itself. Their faces said it all. We had not only lost, but lost to the Giants—a bitter, bitter loss.

Leo the Lip had outdueled Toothpick Charlie, a good name for a rubbed-out character reminiscent of the movie *Some Like It Hot*. And rub us out Leo did. He took great pleasure in the victory, as any opponent would have, but this was the sweetest one of all for him. He had made his mark on baseball as a legendary manager.

Whatever the motives, the Giants had won the pennant, and it was an awfully bitter pill to swallow.

The bus took us back to Ebbets Field. We cleaned out our lockers and scattered like rats.

The season was over, and while we tried to return to normal life, there was no place to hide. Everywhere we went, the loss followed us—like an albatross.

As a result, to this day, that bitterness remains. Duke Snider, in his book *The Duke of Flatbush*, made a sage's worth of observations about that day he was so frustrated. Duke was an icon in Brooklyn, and his name should have been spelled DOOK—in Brooklynese! But nobody was immune from the wrath of the loss. It was doubly bad because of what had happened in the seasons prior to '51. This loss, added to our loss to Philadelphia the year before and the Series loss to the Yankees the year before that, really put the heat on us as a team that couldn't quite win it all. But in the hearts of Dodgers fans, we were "Dem Bums," and they loved us, win or lose.

I think that the unconditional love made life tougher in an ironic way because we knew the love was unconditional and we wanted to reciprocate. Jackie, every year, said he could taste the champagne.

In fact, we were at emotional crossroads at the start of 1952.

As a team, we could have faded into history, but we didn't. We were united in our desire to get back to the postseason once more. We came back stronger than ever in 1952, 1953, 1955, and 1956 and finally won the World Series in 1955.

Sal Yvars, a catcher for the Giants at the time, did an interview for the *Wall Street Journal* a few years ago and said that the Giants had a telescope in the bullpen and a buzzer system to steal signs from our team. I don't know why it took until the new millennium for that story to surface as big news, but it did, and so my response to Sal, on behalf of me and Jackie and the rest of the guys, is in order.

The Dodgers' bench was located on the third-base side at the Polo Grounds, and from that vantage point we faced center field—deep center. The clubhouses were both located in deep center field, with two sets of steps leading up from the bullpens to the clubhouses. On the left side were the visitors, and on the right side were the Giants.

At the top of the steps, and off to the right side, was a window. It was understood by our team that inside that window was Leo Durocher's office. However, that day the window was raised about six inches—enough for a telescope to couch its lens and have a clean view of our pitcher on the mound. The room appeared dark inside, but that probably wouldn't have affected a telescope lens.

"Those dirty birds are probably stealing our signs," we groused. Bobby Thomson never admitted taking, but neither did he deny it.

Ralph Branca agreed with all of us that this was what was happening, but only among us—never publicly—because he didn't want to appear to have sour grapes, and so he faced the reporters and answered their questions without ever mentioning the suspect raised window pane.

Curious as it was, however, at the time, Major League Baseball had, and still has, no rule in its books concerning stealing signs. There wasn't any citywide ordinance in New York at the time prohibiting use of telescopic equipment to aid a ball club in its quest for victory.

Baseball, therefore, was a game in which stealing signs had been a part for many decades, and teams always bragged about their third-base coach's ability to pick up whether a pitcher had a strange motion when he threw a curveball or whether he was coming up too fast in his delivery.

In Chicago's Friendly Confines, Wrigley Field, there was (and is) a huge, manually operated center-field scoreboard with large openings—certainly large enough through which to steal signs. We had no evidence of the fact, but we had our suspicions— which lasted until we headed West.

The Yankees' Bob Turley confided in me that he could steal signs from us at Ebbets Field.

"If I lay down on the dugout steps and kept my eyes level to the ground I could see the tips of Campy's fingers and get your signs," Bob told me.

He probably could, I figured.

Bob was pretty resourceful. But what could he do with the information he collected?

How about the "voice sign," in which a player shouts a key word, like "Heads up" or "Be ready," from the dugout to indicate a fastball or remains silent if a curve is called for. This is a great technique because opposing players hear so much garbage from the opposing dugout that they won't know if a rather innocuous word has any real significance. This is a great ploy often implemented by big-league clubs.

There's also the famous "first-base coach technique," in which the nonchalant first-base coach sees the catcher's signs and relays them to the batter through posture. If he stands up extra straight, a fastball is coming; if he bends over slightly, a curve is on its way.

Some players whom I played alongside didn't want the signs, and some prayed that the catcher would get a bit sloppy and give them a peek at the signs.

Jackie Robinson was one guy who never wanted the signs. He was adamant about it. He felt that any information that could be given to him by the opposition would mess with his mind and ruin his fluidity in the batter's box. It was also dangerous, he told me, because a player ran the risk of relying on falsely planted information. For instance, if a player was told a curve was coming and "looked curve," and the pitcher threw a fastball up and in, the player could get himself killed.

"It takes my guard down," Jackie told me, and he was uncomfortable with the idea that the pitcher might be controlling his thoughts in the batter's box.

He wanted his natural instincts and ability to be unimpaired. He felt he was successful enough so that he didn't need to know the signs. Differing with Jackie on the subject was Carl Furillo, who wanted to know the signs and loved it when he thought he had scooped the pitcher.

The runner on second base would often be told to relay the signs to Carl, who quite often made the pitcher pay for his mistake.

The joke around the clubhouse was that if you gave Carl Furillo the signs, he'd be so happy he'd jump right out of his shoes at the plate. He'd get up at three a.m. and hit a fastball if he knew it was coming.

From a pitcher's standpoint, the most nerve-racking thing that can happen on the mound is when the opposing bench catches you carelessly doing one thing on a fastball and another on a curve and runs at will on you with runners on base.

Clem Labine had a problem that troubled his mind deeply, but Rube Walker was sent to the rescue and straightened him out. Clem used to wrap his curveball grip in an unusual manner, which exposed his wrist below his glove, leaving the hitter to easily pick up the position of his wrist, knowing a curve was coming.

Clem knew that his curve was getting picked off, and he let this get to him.

Rube took Clem on from a different mental state. The best defense, to Rube, was a good offense.

"Clem, quit trying to hide it!" Rube Walker yelled at him.

"Show 'em your curve and the way you go about throwing it, and then throw a nice hard sinker inside and they'll quit trying to steal your signs," he said.

Rube was correct.

The best medicine for a curious hitter was to show the curveball grip and then throw the heat up and inside. It backed them right off the plate. And Clem had to do this only once or twice, and then no one wanted to guess curve on him anymore.

Baseball strategy notwithstanding, a curious event happened right before the infamous Giants playoff. In 1950, Branch Rickey's contract had expired. While to baseball fans that might have been a nonevent, it was quite a significant change in Dodgers history, one that would inevitably alter, and sever, relations between Brooklyn and their beloved Dodgers.

Dressen might have been at the helm as manager in 1951, but times were changing around the front office, and Dressen was our only link to the past.

We no longer had John L. Smith on the board, as he died of cancer. The question of the day was what was going to happen to all of those shares of Dodgers stock he owned.

His widow swiftly answered that question and sold his shares to a young businessman named Walter O'Malley. Little did she realize that she set the stage for two forceful men to become adversaries in the boardroom.

Branch Rickey was told by Major League Baseball that he needed to divest himself if he wanted to move to Pittsburgh and handle Pirates operations. Rickey and O'Malley squared off in a full-scale heavyweight fight—one in which neither man notched a KO. Rickey enlisted the help of his good friend and real estate mogul William Zeckendorf. In the ESPN piece we learned that

Zeckendorf made a phony million-dollar offer to buy the Dodgers, and when O'Malley was forced to trade punches and counter, knowing he was entitled to his commission of 5 percent, William upped the ante to one million and fifty-thousand. O'Malley was conned out of fifty grand, and Rickey was out of the Dodgers organization.

During the press conference, when the transfer of power was made between Rickey and O'Malley, the two exchanged pleasantries. But as Mark A. Reese pointed out in his documentary on the Dodgers, there were ill feelings between the two men, and, as legend had it, O'Malley got a bit lit up that night celebrating and played "Pin the Tail on the Donkey" with Rickey's likeness as the donkey.

6

Back to the Big Show—1952

WHEN SPRING TRAINING STARTED in 1952, we had the best lineup we had in years. Don Newcombe, however, was in the military, overseas in Korea. But a young standout came to the rescue. His name was Joe Black.

As a relief pitcher Joe won fifteen games and saved twenty-five the same year, a phenomenal mark not repeated until Dennis Eckersley made the switch from starter to closer. Joe was just what the doctor ordered that spring in Vero Beach. He had a deceptive fastball and slider, and while many might say that he was a two-pitch pitcher, his control was unbelievable. He could hit the spot where Campy had his glove every time.

Voted Rookie of the Year by the season's end, Joe was the impetus we needed in our rotation to get back to the World Series.

At 6'3", Joe was a true presence on the mound. He gave our rotation some size.

He attributed his opportunity to play pro ball at the major-league level to Jackie Robinson. Jackie had paved the way. And Joe was thankful every minute because he knew how it felt to be denied based on race. He once attended a tryout and was told by a major-league scout that black players couldn't play in the major leagues. Devastated, he ran home and looked through his scrapbook and saw all the faces were white. The scout wasn't lying.

"I tore up all my cards, except for Hank Greenberg!" Joe said after learning that black players weren't allowed to play pro ball.

But Jackie changed all of that. Jackie made it possible for Campy, Newk, Joe, Jim Gilliam, and Sandy Amoros to play in the big leagues.

Joe appreciated Jackie's groundbreaking methods and listened closely to another mentor of his—Roy Campanella. Joe was another direct recipient of the Roy Campanella schooling system, whereby Campy put down the signs and the pitcher threw the ball. No one dared shake him off. I rarely did, and the few times I did—I could count them over my career on one hand—I got burned.

When I didn't, I was always successful, and that was why I always referred to Roy as more than my teammate. Roy was my pal, my confidant, my guiding light out there on the field, and he was a confidant of mine off the field till his dying day.

It didn't take long for Joe Black to love Campy the way I did. All of the veteran pitchers gave Joe the same advice. We told him to listen to Roy, follow whatever he says, and throw with confidence. Jackie agreed. Both Robinson and Campanella took young Joe Black under their wings and made him an instant star. Because of Jackie's perseverance and attitude that life must be made better for all who followed him, Joe was able to help our club get to another World Series.

Just getting back to the World Series caused Duke Snider to remark that he thought this team was more special than it was given credit for, because any team that could go down to the Yankees in five games in '49 and then lose on the last day of the season in '50 and '51 in dramatic, backbreaking losses and still come back to the World Series in 1952 was special beyond mere words. Duke was right on the mark. We were a special club. We were Dodgers. We were a family on spikes. We loved each other and gelled. The fans fueled and stoked our fires. I have never seen a team that could absorb adversity like us and turn the previous year's disaster into the following year's successes. We surprised the baseball world, year in and year out.

The 1952 World Series saw us face the Yanks once more and once again lose, this time in seven games, with every contest being a seesaw. We took the first game; they took the second. We took the third; they took the fourth. Joe Black had been outstanding in the first game, outmatching the Chief, Allie Reynolds. Allie was a perennial postseason winner, but not this time. And so with the Series tied at two games apiece, the scene shifted to the Bronx. The atmosphere was a tense one in the Bronx for Game 5. And little did I know it then that this game was all about the fives.

I was sitting at my locker before Game 5 rummaging through some telegrams. Having lost Game 2, I felt the heat to go out and win one for us. I couldn't get that second-game loss out of my head. Losing to Vic Raschi was bad enough, but losing at Ebbets Field in front of the home faithful, that was too bitter a pill to swallow. I just had to win this game. Sometimes when a person least expects a shooting star, the sky opens up for him.

My shooting star came in the form of a telegram from a friend of mine who was a mayor in a small town in Texas. I had become acquainted with him, and he'd write me as a well-wisher.

The telegram read: "Good luck in Game 5 of the World Series on this fifth day of October, and congratulations on your fifth wedding anniversary."

I thought about it, a bit puzzled. He was correct. This was my fifth wedding anniversary. It was October 5. I was pitching Game 5. Feeling a bit tweaked by the telegram, I jokingly showed it to Red Barber.

Red thought it was more than prophetic. He asked me, "Carl, can I have that wire? I'd like to take it to the booth. It might come in handy."

OK. That was fine with me.

Suddenly, the clock had wound down to the time when I was supposed to be warming up and stretching. I went about my usual routine, having placed the telegram out of my thought process. Jackie always stressed the importance of a clear head for battle.

My buddies gave me an early lead, 4–0, but in the fifth inning I surrendered two cheap runs to the Yankees, and then the Big Cat, Johnny Mize, blasted a three-run homer off me. Five runs in the fifth inning. Now the Yankees had the lead, 5–4. There went the fives. There went my confidence. I knew I was done.

Charlie Dressen emerged from the dugout, hunched over, and walked slowly to the mound. Hodges, Pee Wee, and Jackie came in for a conference, along with Campy.

"Are you alright?" Charlie asked me, taking the ball from me, as is customarily done by managers when the pitcher is being removed for a relief pitcher.

I thought he was nuts for asking me that question. I had just blown the game.

"You surrendered only one hard-hit ball so far," he said to me, referring to the Mize home run.

"Hey, guys! Are you going to make a change or what?" yelled the home-plate umpire as we conversed on the mound.

I sensed the ump's impatience and wondered what in the world Dressen was doing. And then I realized he was stalling for the bullpen. I was so engrossed in my own debacle that I needed to take a step back and think about the fact that the relief guys needed to be warmed up.

"By the way," Charlie asked, "is today your wedding anniversary?"

Now I was totally taken aback.

Here we were at Yankee Stadium in a crucial swing game of the 1952 World Series, not to mention the fact that I just had a disastrous fifth inning, and he's asking me about my marriage! It boggled my mind to the point where I literally went numb on the mound.

"Yes, it is," I said, dumbfounded.

"And is your wife here?" he asked.

"Yes," I answered, knowing now that the bullpen must be ready to come in.

"Charlie, are you making a pitching change or not?" the ump stepped in and asked.

"Are you going to celebrate tonight?" Charlie asked me, referring to my wedding anniversary.

"I had planned to," I told him.

"See if you can get the side out before it gets dark!" he told me and gave me back the ball and walked back to the dugout. I don't know of a manager who ever took the ball from the pitcher and gave it back to him in the same conference without lifting him from the game.

Yogi Berra was up at the plate. He was a tremendous bad-ball hitter. He loved the ball thrown at his shoelaces or high. But I managed to muster the strength to fly out to right. I escaped the inning without allowing any more runs. But we were still down 5–4. I thought Charlie had just let me finish the inning in order to use a pinch hitter. If I were the manager, I would have probably taken myself out of the game, but thank God he was in charge and showed great confidence in me.

I was due up to hit in the top of that inning, and so I knew I was done.

"You're hitting," he told me.

Had he lost his mind?

I went up to hit and stayed in the game. My sixth inning was a good one, and we tied the game in the seventh. Now both teams had at five runs. Talk about the luck of the fives!

I stayed in that game the whole way. In the eleventh inning Duke Snider doubled in a run for us to give us the lead, and I put the Yankees away in the bottom half of the inning to ensure the victory. The last batter was Yogi Berra, and I struck him out to win the game for us, but on my last pitch to him I burst a blister on my finger and couldn't throw effectively again that Series.

A sportswriter told me that I had thrown a total of nine no-hit innings in an eleven-inning victory, and I had retired the final nineteen batters in a row!

Meanwhile, up in the booth Vin Scully and Barber were amazed with the story of my telegram and the fives. Scully said that he looked at the clock out in the outfield in Yankee Stadium after Berra struck out: it read 5:05 p.m.

Our team came home to Brooklyn, fans cheering their lungs out for us, leading the Big Bad Bombers 3–2 in games, and after such an emotional win one might have thought the Yankees were dead.

The Yankees once again proved that, like a top-notch boxing heavyweight, they are most dangerous when on the ropes.

They rebounded with a fury that would have been fit for a battlefield in ancient Greece. They took Game 6 from us at Ebbets Field, setting the stage for a whirlwind Game 7.

Game 7. A nemesis once again fleeces us dry. Mickey Mantle did his usual; he blasted a home run. Suddenly, in the blink of an eye, the New York Yankees had another World Series trophy.

Although our team wasn't intimidated by the Yankees, we couldn't break that invisible barrier and win the World Series.

And my kids still used their 1952 Mickey Mantle Bowman cards to scale into a dish, a card-tossing contest as old as the rectangular pieces of gum that came with the baseball cards, and to put in their bicycle spokes. There was no such thing as collecting back then. Cards were bought in packs from the ice cream truck that came by, and they had that rectangular piece of hard gum. It was all done for the sheer joy of it.

In fact, when I recently told some reporter for *Sports Collector's Digest* that I didn't even have a 1952 card of myself for my own children, fans started sending me some to keep. We just didn't hang onto that stuff because nobody thought it was valuable. The only thing of value to us was the ring—the World Series ring we so desperately wanted.

So, we gave them the fight of their lives. And we knew we'd be back stronger than ever in 1953.

Once again, in 1953, the fat lady sang, but she sang only for the New York Yankees.

Spring training was vastly different that year.

Charlie Dressen had ideas, visions, and a new lineup for the team.

He changed the lineup.

At first I thought I misheard.

"What is he thinking?" I asked myself when I found out in Vero Beach that we really had a new lineup.

But Charlie had a new weapon—Jim Gilliam.

Jackie was moved to third base because they thought his range was fading. I didn't agree with the reasoning, but the results were terrific.

Jim promptly led off with a burst of energy, leading the league in doubles and not relinquishing that lead. He scored 125 runs that season—and when we needed them most. For me, the '53 season was terrific because I won twenty games. But my twentieth win didn't come the usual way.

We had clinched the pennant in Milwaukee, and I won my nineteenth game that year with the victory. That should have been the end of my season, as Charlie was trying to limber up the rookies and most of the clubs were playing the second-stringers against us the rest of the way through.

However, Charlie gave me one more start, and before the start there was a team meeting.

"I'm playing the regular lineup today," Dressen announced. "I want you guys to go out there and get Erskine his twentieth win."

Now Charlie was not known for having a soft spot. He was no sentimental man. But he liked my work ethic enough to want to get me my twentieth.

Once again, the team camaraderie took over and gave us that injection of strength upon which we drew every time adversity stared us down.

I won my twentieth and actually could have made a few more starts, but I was only used to keep me ready for the postseason.

In the '53 World Series we again squared off against the Yankees and again lost to them, this time in six games. And I got my first postseason lesson on never hitting a player trying to knock him down.

I know that pitchers are ordered by team managers, as I was by Charlie Dressen, to flatten hitters. They wanted a good knockdown, about neck high behind the hitter. They didn't want the hitters hit, because that would have put them on base, but they wanted them dusted off the plate. These orders are not implied orders; they are real directives with the intent to send a batter upside down.

Managers deny it all the time, but it is a fact. Ever since the stitches have been sewn on a baseball in red, managers have ordered pitchers to "protect your own hitters."

Of all the settings to fire up the team we least wanted to fire up, this was a pickle. Right before Game 3, I was summoned to meet with Dressen. Charlie more or less accosted me for a "discussion," which turned out to be a filibuster by him.

"This is Ebbets Field," he started in on me.

"Berra is dug in to his ankles in that batter's box! He can't even see his shoes!" he continued without letting me get a word in edgewise.

"This guy has got to go down! This is an order! I want him upside down!"

That was the end of it. There was no time for rebuttal on my part. He had walked away.

Dressen's discussion with me was officially over at the turn of his uniform, his back facing me and already yards ahead in stride. Case closed. I had my orders.

Get a strike on Berra and then put him on his back.

When I left that discussion, I wasn't quite as enthusiastic about this idea as Dressen himself was—but I knew I had to carry it out. If I didn't, I'd have to pay for it.

Yogi came up to bat and dug himself into the batter's box, just as Charlie predicted. But to me, that didn't symbolize anything foreboding. I thought the best medicine was a good strikeout. But I knew my orders.

I carried out my assignment with the delicacy of a bull in a china shop. I had the first part of the equation down pat—getting a strike on Yogi. It was the second part where things went awry. I didn't want to hit Yogi, but I knew Charlie wanted me to loosen him up with the knockdown pitch.

My first try was a valiant one. I reared back and threw a pretty good fastball inside, but the pitch went about chest high on Yogi, and he didn't move a muscle. He just raised his arm and the ball hit him in the ribs. I could hear him groaning at home plate, and he took first base without even a glance at me.

Dressen wasn't happy, and neither was I. I was mad as all get-out at Dressen. Yogi, I know, was furious inside, but he didn't show it. Not yet.

"I didn't want him on first base!" Dressen yelled at me inside the dugout after the inning was over.

"Next time he's up with no one on base, get a strike on him and do it right!" Charlie instructed me in a not-so-calm manner.

I followed Dressen's instructions to the letter of the law—his law—once more. The next time Yogi came up to the plate, I promptly got a first-pitch strike and then once again tried the knockdown.

This was where I once more went afoul.

The knockdown was up and in—but did Yogi go down? No! He turned away and the ball struck him solidly on the right elbow—and this time he glared at me all the way as he walked to first base.

It just went to prove me right. Yogi killed us in that Series. He was so mad at us—and Dressen—that he ended up hitting .429 in the Series. When I next saw the good-natured Yogi, he only grinned and said to me in his deep, soft voice, "Carl, were you throwing at me?"

My philosophy has always been that once you rattle someone's insides by knocking him down, he will get up and bring it back to you full throttle. A .220 hitter becomes a .400 hitter on the next pitch.

I did end up striking out fourteen batters to win the game for us, so Yogi didn't hurt me in that particular game. But in principle I was right. He helped their comeback efforts. I felt I needed to notch this win because I had lost Game 1 of the Series for us, but we didn't need to rile up the entire Yankees bench and awaken the sleeping lions, which as '51 showed us could prove disastrous.

We lost that World Series, but once again, every game was close and well fought. Solid pitching and timely hitting were the medicines of the day for both teams. Cox and Gilliam hit home runs for us in Game 5, but the Yankees rebounded in that game with home runs from Mickey Mantle, Gene Woodling, Billy Martin, and Gil McDougald. They allowed on average four to five runs a game. We allowed four to five runs a game. The pitching was the same with respect to ERA; just the losses columns were different. Still, there was no domination as far as I'm concerned; we equaled them hit for hit, homer for homer. They had fifty-six hits and nine homers. We gobbled up sixty-four hits and had eight homers.

7
Wait Till Next Year

"HEY, WAIT TILL NEXT YEAR, guys. We'll get 'em!" a loyal Bums fan shouted as we departed from the field after yet another World Series loss to the Yankees in 1953.

The look on Jackie's face said it all. He winced as if in pain every time somebody would use that expression. The skin on the bridge of his nose would fold inward and form a look that announced he was either sad or mad. It was a look of unexplained pain, as if he had just lost a loved one, and so one time I pressed the issue.

"Jackie, what's wrong?" I whispered privately, out of earshot of the other players. "You really hate that phrase, but why?"

I *had* to know. After all, we were all upset about 1951, and we were upset that things didn't go our way in '52, but his grimace seemed personal, very personal.

"Carl, it's the same every year. Whether it's our team or civil rights, it's always the same. It's not the phrase so much as what it says about our country," Jackie explained.

Get prepared. Be ready. Deliver.

This was the Robinson way.

Jackie was always prepared, always ready. He delivered for us countless times on the field—and he was a clutch postseason player.

He felt the country had not lived up to its end of the bargain. It was almost as if society was a faceless entity dragging its feet on matters that were important to the advancement of African Americans.

"It's the end of 1953, Carl, and some of the hotels around the league still won't allow us to stay with you guys when we go there. It's *always* 'wait till next year.' Carl, we've got to be persistent, you know that. We've got to change things in '54."

Society was moving at the pace of a small, ill snail. Some stadiums outside of New York were still in the Dark Ages. It was not until the early fifties that the segregated stands began to disappear. St. Louis was still segregating fans—blacks were allowed to sit only in the right-field pavilion. Cincinnati had segregated stands until the practice was discontinued in 1954. Ignorance had run the bases for so long south of the Mason-Dixon Line that the desegregation that *was* taking place in the early fifties at St. Louis's Sportsman's Park was a sure sign that "next year" was starting to happen.

As a lad, Pee Wee Reese grew up in the segregated state of Kentucky. He knew lots of African Americans but hadn't worked side by side with them before. Playing alongside Jackie was a new experience for him. Pee Wee disliked the idea of judging people based on their race; he was as egalitarian as the day was long. He was uneasy about the fact that Jackie was being mistreated by the rival teams and their fans. He walked over to Jackie at Crosley Field in Cincinnati in 1947 and in front of the booing fans and news media put his hand on Jackie's shoulder, publicly demonstrating his acceptance of Jackie Robinson as his teammate and comrade. As the team captain, Pee Wee sent a message not only to the Dodgers players, some of whom had doubts at the beginning about Jackie, but to the entire league that he was on Jackie's side in this battle for racial equality. Pee Wee's gesture in Cincinnati that day was a pat on the back not just for Jackie but for baseball—the game needed that show of good faith so that society could see what it was doing wrong.

The 1954 baseball season saw old friends reunited and social strides made. Jackie, Campy, and Newk were back together again on one ball field, and the Chase Park Hotel in St. Louis abolished its racist policies.

This was also the year I had been involved in a bet and didn't even know it until it was almost all over.

I had been making eighteen thousand dollars a year in 1953, the year I won twenty games. I was sure that Buzzy was going to give me a raise in 1954.

Hank Greenberg, the legendary Detroit Tigers Hall of Famer, was the general manager of the Cleveland Indians at that time, and he bet Bavasi ten dollars that Buzzy wouldn't give me what I asked for. Then he told me all about the friendly little wager between the two of them. Amused at first, I decided to rattle Buzzy's cage a bit and try to sneak away with a win late in the game.

I approached Buzzy to renegotiate my contract before the start of the 1954 season.

"What do you want?" Buzzy asked me in the hotel lobby in Atlanta where the winter meetings were taking place.

"I want thirty thousand dollars," I said matter-of-factly, looking Buzzy straight in the eye as if I had this money coming to me.

"Carl, I can't do that," he said. "Walter O. would fire me."

"OK, then pay Greenberg!" I told him.

"Now wait a minute!" Buzzy continued. "Let's talk."

"Here's what I'll do," Buzzy said as if he had the deal of the century for me. "Twenty-eight thousand, five hundred is as far as I can go, but I'll make you a deal. You bring your family to spring training, and let me pick up their expenses—there's your thirty thousand dollars."

"Not quite," I retorted. "That usually costs me less than a thousand dollars. Buzzy, how about paying for the dental work I'm having done in Anderson in the winter?" I asked him.

He finally relented. My dentist loved getting those Dodgers checks, and I was satisfied with my six gold inlays.

Spring training in 1954 started off with two missions: one a team mission, the other a personal one for Jackie. We also had another new skipper, as a shy, pacifistic man named Walter Alston took the helm.

The team mission was obvious—get to the World Series and then beat the accursed Yanks and bring Brooklyn a long-awaited championship.

When we headed north from spring training I was besieged by reporters in Washington, D.C., at the Shoreham Hotel.

"What's wrong with him?" they asked me in the hotel about Alston, because I was the player rep.

"He doesn't say much. He's not giving us anything to print," they complained as a group.

Walter was an interesting character because a player always knew where he stood with him; but if a situation didn't need embellishing, Walter didn't embellish. He'd just say "yes" or "no" and give one-word answers, a nightmare for a reporter. His passive attitude bothered Jackie, who thought Alston should have protected his players more on the field, and while he always kept his attitude toward the manager respectful, the emotions spilled over in Chicago when we were playing the Cubs.

Duke Snider had hit what we all thought was a home run to left center. The ball caromed off a fan and came down onto the field. It was ruled a double by the second-base umpire. The ump said it hit off the fence and came back into fair play. Jackie left the dugout and charged the umpire, vehemently disagreeing. But he was all alone out there without a manager by his side. Jackie became furious.

"You don't protect your players!" he raced into the dugout and yelled at Alston.

"You sit there like a bump on a log!" he continued, storming in the dugout. This was one of the few times an all-star player chided

his manager in front of an entire team, but Jackie had high standards and thought Walter should have been out there raising his voice and defending us.

"I thought the call was right," Walter responded to a dumbfounded dugout.

The incident showed me how baseball is a game not only of inches but of split-second perception, and more important, how Jackie really did bottle up his enthusiasm during those first two years.

In '54 Jackie's personal mission went a lot smoother in hindsight, compared to trying to get Walter animated, and that was bringing the Chase Park Hotel up to modern baseball speed—one hotel, one locker room, and allowing African Americans to stay there.

For Newk, the "Home from Korea" welcome mat was less than swept clean. No reservations allowed at the Chase Park Hotel. Contrary to how the Chase Park Hotel might be perceived now, in its day it was the envy of most hotels, with its exceptionally high ratings and its countless amenities for guests—white guests, that is.

Don Newcombe had been over in Korea risking his life for our country. Outspoken as he was, when he returned home to find that progress was happening but at about the pace of a turtle, he was none too pleased.

After all, here was a young man, only twenty-seven at the start of the 1954 season, who had won seventeen, nineteen, and twenty games, respectively, his first three seasons in the big leagues and then lost two prime years to military service.

It didn't take long for Newk to find out that he could come home from the turrets overseas to find the same segregated hotels back here in the States. And his unhappiness was loud, clear, and in no uncertain terms.

But in St. Louis at that time, segregation was in full force. Baseball wasn't being singled out by the hotel, and neither were

Jackie and Newk. It didn't make swallowing the situation any easier, but they had their ideology and weren't going to change overnight.

They had their ideology, their rules, and their swimming pool.

"Look, Newk, you're bitter, I'm bitter, but we're going to take the *I* out of bitter and replace it with an *E*," a confident Robinson told young Don Newcombe.

They calmly approached the manager of this five-star hotel and asked why the hotel was off-limits to African-American patrons.

"It's the swimming pool, guys," he bluntly told them.

"The swimming pool?" queried Jackie.

"Look, we can't have you guys in or around the pool," the manager informed them. "It's a place where everybody socializes."

It dawned on both Jackie and Newk that this swimming pool had some deep social significance that lay at the root of racism. Prodded by the idea that they had nothing to lose by querying further, they did so.

"We're not swimmers," Newk said. "We're ballplayers. All we want to do is stay with our team and go out and play baseball."

The manager thought about it—and a decision was made. The last Confederate flag was lowered to half-staff, although not actually removed from the flagpole. We often went to see Lena Horne, a regular nightclub performer at the Chase Park who had been refused a hotel room there. This too finally changed—and all because of Jackie and Newk.

Robinson and Newk had won their case in court—the people's court.

Although the African-American players were still not allowed to eat in the dining room and had their meals brought to their rooms, Jackie assured Newk that slow change was better than none and that he needed to be patient. And he was right. The very next season the Chase Park declared its dining room open to all.

Everything would be changing in due time, but due time was what made the strongest of men lose their hair from angst. It was rather ironic that this calmness and tranquilizing attitude came from the same man who had paid regular visits to the mound to agitate Newk whenever Newk got into a jam. This was Jackie's method of getting Newk to step up his game.

Those seemingly pithy words Jackie once told me—get prepared and be ready—seemed now as complex as a man's soul and emotions. I realized that he was preparing not only the country for change but himself for the process of bringing about the change. Robinson shined in these tough situations because his sharp mind and sometimes sharp tongue always got the point across—and in a seemingly irrefutable way.

I can personally attest to Jackie's consistency in all aspects of his life—his devotion to baseball, his devotion to God, and his devotion to his family and to civil rights.

Another incident in 1954, although unpublicized, provided me further proof of Jackie's tenacity. It took place at Cincinnati's Crosley Field, on a scorching Sunday afternoon, when Jackie was the maddest I had ever seen him. It centered on getting prepared—or not being prepared, as the case was that day.

Crosley had power alleys of 382 feet in left and 383 feet in right, with a dead center field of 390 feet. Situated near a marvelous domed train station, the ballpark was accessible to local townspeople and deep Southerners alike—a railroad crossroads of the Midwest. In the summertime, the on-field temperatures at Crosley Field rocketed to ninety degrees with the ease of a lazy fly ball. On the Superior Towel & Linen Service Building across the street was a sign that read, "HIT THIS SIGN AND WIN A SIEBLER SUIT." It was reminiscent of our own Abe Stark sign back at Ebbets Field.

The particular Sunday afternoon in question started off innocuous enough with our usual team bus ride to the ballpark from the Netherland Plaza Hotel. Jackie was pumped for the game, much the way he was pumped for every game, and whom we were playing didn't matter to him. He just wanted to win. How we fared against them in the past, who was pitching that day, or the weather—all were inconsequential. Jackie was ready to take on the world with the same gusto that one would summon to devour a seven-course meal. I don't think I ever met anyone quite as ready and focused as Jackie Robinson in my life in baseball.

We took the first game of that day's doubleheader, and we were hoping for the double-dip sweep.

Minutes before our team took the field in the second game, however, a black man from the stands summoned Jackie.

"Where's my Jackie?" the fan asked in a rather boisterous voice.

There had been a series of excursion trains from the South bringing groups of African-American fans to see Jackie Robinson play. The groups were from Birmingham, Atlanta, and other Southern metropolises, and they all made that sojourn to see Jackie because of what he meant to their future. Every African-American fan saw a glimmer of sunshine through Jackie Robinson and what Jackie represented.

This particular fan had obviously left home dressed to the hilt, but his clothes were now in disarray. His gait was less than even. His speech was slurred, and it didn't take Jackie long to notice that the fan was intoxicated. This infuriated Jackie.

"Get out of my face, you slob!" Robinson tore into him as he approached. "I bet your front yard looks as bad as you do. Go home and clean up!"

The man was stopped dead in his tracks by Jackie's piercing voice and words. He made a sudden about-face and disappeared into the swelling crowd.

Jackie dealt with that man the same way he dealt with all members of his race who, in his mind, demeaned themselves or showed a lack of dignity. To Jackie, it was necessary for everyone to hold themselves up with dignity if a truly equal America was to be accomplished. The fan, and everyone else who heard Jackie's response, got the message.

This was indeed the maddest I had ever seen Jackie—worse than when the fans threw a black cat onto the field in Philadelphia.

I wanted to know from Jackie himself why this man had angered him so much.

The difference between this incident and the Ben Chapman incidents in Philadelphia was, as Jackie explained to me, rather simple.

Ben Chapman had ordered his pitchers in 1947 to throw at Jackie Robinson, as Robin Roberts has confirmed. In fact, there was originally a hefty fine if a Phillies pitcher didn't throw at Robinson. One day Richie Ashburn, their all-star center fielder, got into Chapman's face and said, "Every time you have our pitchers throw at him, he gets a huge hit to beat us." Chapman thought about it and then instituted a fine for anyone who did throw at Jackie by the end of 1948. But the feelings inside the hearts of Ben Chapman and the partisan crowds in Philadelphia didn't vanish, they just became tucked away because times were changing.

"I can't control Ben Chapman," Jackie said to me near the end of 1948. "He's going to say what he wants and they'll throw at me. But what I can do is instill some pride in my race through perseverance."

Jackie felt he could instill a sense of pride in African Americans around the country and lead them in the cause for civil rights. That fan in Cincinnati represented an impediment to that civil rights cause. Jackie said the man's behavior was just as damaging to the furthering of civil rights as anything.

"He's not ready for the day," Jackie told me with sweat on his brow, seconds after his outburst. "We need to be prepared, Carl, not drunk."

Get prepared. Be ready. Deliver.

But I learned early on that politics was not the fuel that stoked Jackie's fire. Jackie was not political in nature. He sought out those in power who supported an equal America, and it didn't matter which party they were affiliated with; if they espoused these virtues, Robinson was with them. President Eisenhower disappointed Jackie because he had a "wait till next year" philosophy, and so Jackie embraced the more passionate Hubert Humphrey, who seemed to have a deep sense of urgency toward civil rights and who promised sweeping changes if elected.

Although the critical New York media was instrumental in Jackie's Rookie of the Year Award in 1947, they also fed his enthusiasm.

There was a wide array of newspaper writers at the time — among them Leonard Koppett, Roscoe McGowen, John Dribbinger, and Dick Young. This was as eclectic a group of men as any room could handle at one time. McGowen and Dribbinger of the *New York Times* were as well respected as columnists could be at that time — and they could have written with the best in any era. Leonard Koppett was a Hall of Fame writer who believed in the printed word. He was an honorable man. He was on the side of Jackie Robinson. And then there were those writers who were out to find a good story — rile up the locker room, throw some gasoline on the fire.

This was the post-gag-order era. Jackie was now "Mr. Quotable" and he let the guys know when he thought things weren't just so. He was not about to back down from controversy when his heart told him that standing up was the right thing to do.

But in the process of becoming the most-quoted athlete around, often he became the most-misquoted athlete around.

Hot copy or not, Jackie kept up with everything in the papers on a daily basis. I know today the players may say that they don't "look at the papers," but Jackie did — and I think the players today do, too — as we all did. Only Jackie had more good reason to know what words were being put in his mouth.

Jackie read every edition of all seven of the New York papers — so to say he was well informed is an understatement.

The *New York Daily News* had an interesting sportswriter at the time — a Dodgers beat writer — who sometimes took exception to Jackie's remarks. Usually, beat reporters follow the team and print stories about the team in a noncontroversial way. But Dick Young was a writer who played hardball with the pen.

I'll never forget the day Dick approached Jackie's locker and asked him, "Why when I talk to Campy is it always baseball, and when I talk to you it's always civil rights and displeasure with some aspect of society?" That was typical Dick Young.

I was astonished that Dick would try to get into a subject as sensitive as this with Jackie. But his sense of timing — or lack thereof — made me wonder how Jackie would respond.

Although it was well known that Campy and Jackie had distinct opinions on the subjects and had different manners of expression, and each was entitled to his way of looking at his own life and experiences leading to the big leagues, Dick Young treaded on thin ice with this question.

But Jackie — to his credit — took the high road. He wasn't mad. He just explained to Dick his point of view. Jackie felt that his experience in the big leagues was meant to make life — not just baseball — better for the next generation. He viewed the game as a microcosm of what society could accomplish. Dick understood — or at least nodded that he did.

Roy Campanella was not as much a social activist. He was a man who had come from the streets of Philadelphia and had to endure the Negro Leagues, Mexico, South America, and Cuba and felt that his journey to the majors was so long and tedious that he wanted only to have fun every day. His constant smile was genuine because he was glad to be in the majors and wanted no part of controversy in any shape or form. Both men were right in their approach because no man can, or should, tell another how to feel about life—especially that person's own life. Each man had experiences that molded his own personality. And each man was entitled to feel his own way about coping with racial inequality in America.

The differences in philosophy between Jackie and Campy were real, but they never became an issue on or off the field. Each held to his own personal views, and each respected the other's views.

Jackie just felt the cause inside him. He wanted to be recognized as a patriotic American first, and then as an African American. He was not about what the world could do for him but about being ready to change the world, and when he saw something not right he thought he owed it to himself and the next generation to speak his mind.

Jackie often told me that he wished society could be like baseball. Baseball, in his view, was more advanced than society—more connected. Baseball gave men an even chance. Baseball allowed dreams to be realized.

Jackie Robinson truly believed in America. He was a patriot first and a ballplayer second. He loved our Constitution and thought that America fell short of the breadth of that Constitution. He had an innate "let's do it" attitude about him, but much to his chagrin America wasn't as fired up as he was. And while Campy and Jackie had two very distinct philosophies about their roles as major-league African-American ballplayers, they kept their disagreements private. Jackie saw a bigger picture and carried a heavier load. Making the team, for him, was simply the means to much larger and more national ends.

In 1954 it was as if history wanted both teams to have a respite from the battlefields. It was meant to be that way. The fans were given a chance to wipe the dirt kicked up from the hard slides off their clothing.

In the '54 World Series, Bob Lemon, Early Wynn, Mike Garcia, Bob Feller, Larry Doby, and the rest of the Cleveland Indians squared off against Sal Maglie, Willie Mays, and the rest of Durocher's New York Giants. While the Giants swept the best pitching staff in the majors that October, the Yankees and the Dodgers were sitting at home wondering why they had fallen short of another rematch.

We fished in the off-season and cleaned our rods, hoping that the next year, instead of a striped bass, we'd catch ourselves a World Series trophy.

8

Our Year Had Come

OUR YEAR HAD FINALLY COME — 1955 made all of those brides-maid years well worth it. Maturing along the way, we grew up with the townsfolk in Brooklyn, learning that life was not about the ends. Life, after all, was all about the journey. It was about all of those road trips that seemed to never end, the Pullman cars that seemed like horizontal sardine cans. Life was all about the pit stops, the mad dashes toward home and the mad dashes to get a milkshake.

We had made our marks and measured ourselves against the walls of success, much as a parent marks a wall when a child is growing up.

The years of 1949, 1951, 1952, 1953, and 1954 were important for our team. We men grew together with regard to both team chemistry and psyche. We jelled in the locker room. Our families were close. We raised our kids together.

Winning had also brought us together. Beliefs brought us together. And togetherness was what saw us through the tough times and what prepared us for the end of the baseball journey — the 1955 World Series championship.

Every time I stroll down memory lane, all of the infield dust tastes as gritty as it did fifty years ago.

I also take umbrage with some recent revisionist history, specifically when it comes to our rival New York Yankees.

There's always someone who sums up the Yankees' victories in the postseason as thus: "The Yankees dominated the Dodgers." Not true!

In my eyes, that summation has a faulty premise. It just wasn't that way fifty years ago.

"I'm not going to ever admit the Yankees dominated us!" I told a reporter in June of 2004, when the Yankees and Mets squared off at the summer's start for six classic Subway Series games.

"I just won't ever say it because it's not true."

A team doesn't make a World Series in 1949, 1952, 1953, 1955, and 1956 and get dominated. The Yankees won all but one of the World Series—1955—but they never dominated us.

Domination refers to the idea of one team beating and embarrassing another team. Not so in our case—and I intend to win this case in this literary court.

We dominated the National League just as the Yankees dominated the American League. The leagues at that point in history had eight teams each. We were atop our league year in and year out. Likewise, they were atop their league on a yearly basis.

Back then there wasn't any wild-card or multidivisional playoff format. There wasn't any expansion. Expansion happened for the first time in '61. No, this battle of the dynasties was clearly a case of the best and brightest squaring off in World Series after World Series, nearly every year from 1952 through 1956.

Fittingly so, 1955 belonged to *us*. It was always *us* versus *them*.

The New York Yankees represented the pomposity of superiority. They believed in themselves as much as their fans believed in them. They were real pros, with a sprinkle of arrogance.

Their uniforms were pristine, and their ballpark was big and foreboding. The facade was regal, like that of the Colosseum in Rome, and the bleachers were so far out in left center that a home run there was the inside-the-park variety.

Even their players had brassy names and brassier marquees. The billboards were just a bit bigger in the Big Bad Bronx. The hot dog vendors screamed just a bit louder. The fans were just a bit more sophisticated. Their coffee machines lasted forever, and so did the commercials.

No Yankees fan would ever wipe his mouth on his sleeve after a good hot dog. No Yankees fan would ever misspell the name of his or her favorite player. The fans in the Bronx spoke English, not Brooklynese.

But our pitcher, Johnny Podres, must have had an angel on his shoulder helping him along the way in '55 because he ate that all-star lineup for lunch and wiped them on his shirtsleeves for dinner. It was a long time coming. After all, the Yankees had their days in the sun, first in '49, and then in '51, '52, and '53.

And decades later, Jackie told the press how he felt about the insinuation that there was an air of Yankees domination. He not only refuted it but blasted back with both barrels.

Jackie had become involved in a rather heated newspaper war with Jim Murray of the *Los Angeles Times* during his playing days. He let Jim know loud and clear that Casey Stengel was not a good manager and that he won only because he had the horses. Jackie thought Casey was a clown and not an astute manager.

Jim Murray took exception to these remarks and wrote about the topic in his column, pointing to Casey's stats as manager of a five-in-a-row World Series victor. Jackie pointed to the talent he had on his club.

For a period of time the crossfire was answered through the print media. Murray wrote through his column, and Jackie responded through the New York media. And the media war was on, which went to prove that the Dodgers and Yankees took their rivalry seriously, right down to the spirit of the pen.

The Yankees were the champions of the business world.

We, on the other hand, were the people's champions.

Jackie and I saw it in the eyes of the schoolkids whenever we paid visits to the various classrooms around the city.

We had a great time interacting with the kids—talking to them about good sportsmanship, character building, not being afraid of failure, and the importance of education. We drew on our own backgrounds and where we had come from to illustrate the point that achieving dreams is possible, but only if you follow the straight and narrow. The kids always listened and always enjoyed our talks. It wasn't different from what they heard at home, but when they heard it from a legend like Robinson, it meant the world to them.

The waters were calm that spring of 1955 in Vero Beach when I fished there. Nature certainly belied what was to come that season once we headed north from the sunny east coast of Florida.

This was a special time in baseball history. Throughout the annals, few teams stand out as people's choices. I was privileged enough to have grabbed the rosin bag quite a few times over my long career with this team. Every year we thought about how long it would take for "next year" to come. Every spring we heard the encouragement from the Dodgertown faithful, the "you'll get 'em this year." It was as if the seasons were played in fast-forward so that we could just get back to the World Series.

But before the champagne was poured and the smiles plastered all over our boyish faces could be captured by the photographers, the season needed to have a poignant moment.

That defining moment was Pee Wee Reese's thirtieth birthday party—July 22, 1955. The pregame barely differed from the norm. The swelling crowds bustled and catcalled as usual.

However, at the end of the fifth inning, when the game becomes official, we had our on-the-field party for Pee Wee. Vin Scully and Happy Felton served as emcees. President Dwight D. Eisenhower and commissioner Ford Frick had sent personal messages that were read aloud on the PA system. New York Governor Harriman and General Douglas MacArthur sent messages as well that were read aloud for the capacity crowd on hand to celebrate Pee Wee and join in the big party.

I presented Pee Wee with a silver tray with the autographs of all of his teammates engraved on it. Pee Wee's wife, Dottie, and daughter, Barbie, were on the field next to Pee Wee, and when the center-field gate opened, out streamed a line of cars—one by one, parading down the dirt perimeter of the ballpark.

As they passed home plate a huge fishbowl containing keys was held out for Barbie, and when Barbie reached into the fishbowl, she drew the Chevrolet.

The finale: a huge birthday cake was rolled out, the lights dimmed, and the capacity crowd of thirty-four thousand fans lit matches. Organist Gladys Gooding led the fans in singing "Happy Birthday" to their favorite Dodger. The celebration ended, and we took the field in the top of the sixth to finish the game.

No one could have predicted what would ensue at the top of the sixth inning when the lights were turned back on. It might as well have been July Fourth, what with the fireworks that took place after the game in our clubhouse.

The grounds crew, in their own special way, decided to pay tribute to the "Little Colonel" from Louisville. They had climbed the roof to where the eight pennants representing the eight teams in our National League flew and removed them. In their places stood eight Confederate flags—to honor Pee Wee.

The game ended with a Dodgers win, but a livid Jackie Robinson stormed into the clubhouse. A few of us tried to console him, but it was to no avail. In Jackie's heart it was as if Jim Crow had opened up the gate to center field and trotted in to play, mitt in hand. Jackie saw the Confederate flags as representing an evil empire—an empire against human dignity and racial equality. However, the flags weren't put up by the grounds crew for racist reasons but out of innocent affection for Pee Wee. Nevertheless, Jackie was about as hot as I'd seen him because he felt this was an indignity done to him right in his own home—Ebbets Field.

The good times did roll along that summer, as we ended up winning the pennant with a resounding resolve to "win it all" this time around against the Yankees, and Newk was back in full form with another twenty-win season.

Along the way, the Robinson knack for psyching out the opponent shone bright in Chicago one day. Jackie had Sam "Toothpick" Jones of the Chicago Cubs, a hard thrower with a nasty curve, in a fluster at Wrigley Field.

He knew just what to yell at Sam when he was standing inside the batter's box.

"You can't get me out, you big slob! Throw the ball over!"

Sam was so flustered that he got wider with every pitch.

Jackie ended up on first base, and then the Robinson show was in full swing.

"You can't pick me off! I'll steal second on you!" Robinson shouted to the pitcher's mound from first base, knowing this would really put Jones over the edge.

And after a few throws home, Robinson ran on Jones and stole second base.

Jackie was in his zone now.

He was always in the game, physically and verbally. He paralyzed Sam Jones that day, stealing third and then home. Sam threw down his toothpick in disgust. It was a harbinger of the Dodgers' ability to take it all that fall.

The Yankees had their own mystique, and we wanted to show we were tough enough to finally conquer it.

We couldn't wait to get the season over and face the Yankees in the World Series. Only this time, things would be different. We had bolstered our pitching staff mid-season by bringing up Roger Craig and Don Bessent. Alston conducted a series of strong clubhouse meetings to prepare us for the Big Dance. It was no understatement that we felt we needed this World Series championship to prove to the world that these Dodgers were true champions.

Jackie was in rare form, and he knew that this would be one of the last chances he'd have at a World Series championship.

Jackie always did his "I might steal home today" dance down the third-base line. The 1955 World Series was no exception.

Whitey Ford was on the mound for the New York Yankees, and once again Jackie kept moving off third base, taking big strides and moving back and forth from side to side. Ford gave Jackie a couple of looks and began his delivery. Jackie took off—not bluffing this time. In what seemed like a split second, he raced toward home. The throw arrived simultaneously. Yogi didn't have to reach for the ball—it was right there. Jackie was tagged just as he made contact with home plate, gliding into a very low slide with only his right toe crossing the front edge of home plate and his body toward the infield. Yogi's glove went down, and so did umpire Bill Stewart's arms—with hands held flat, indicating safe. Jackie had stolen home. He had done the unbelievable in a World Series, and Yogi went into orbit. He stomped around home plate out of his mind, but nothing was changing the mind of Stewart. Jackie was safe.

From our bench on the third-base side of Yankee Stadium we could not tell just how close it was. Yogi clearly thought he had tagged Jackie out.

Looking down at the play as the hitter, Frank Kellert, did, Jackie must have looked out, because when the writers asked Kellert about the play, he surprised the world by saying he thought Jackie was out. Jackie was none too pleased with Kellert's remarks.

In replays of the black-and-white footage, taken from the ground vantage point, it appears that Jackie deftly slid under the tag and was safe.

Yogi was far away from our bench, and so we couldn't hear what he was yelling at Stewart, but the Incredible Hulk in Yogi was ever present as he jumped up and down around the umpire, yelling everything in the book at him.

The funnier part of the story is that to this day, Yogi still believes, and says openly, that Jackie was out. We think umpire Bill Stewart was right.

Jackie was the quickest man on the bases I ever saw. He just had the intangible instincts that cannot be taught. He knew when to take the lead, how far off first or third to position himself, and exactly when to head out for the steal.

A harbinger of the sweet taste of the bubbly to come, the call stood.

Jackie and the rest of us were on our way to meet Destiny face-to-face. The fans prayed for our victory in every game, in every inning, and in every swing of our bats.

We won the World Series in a dramatic seventh game. Sandy Amoros made a now-legendary spectacular running catch down the left-field line in the sixth inning to shut down a Yankees rally. From September 28 to October 4, New York was a baseball city. We talked baseball over the dinner table and at the breakfast table the next day. We dreamed baseball dreams that were no different this year from the other years. But this year the dreams came true. We pinched each other, and we woke up winners.

The games were exciting, but unlike the annual in-season Subway Series between the Mets and Yankees that are played today, the games meant everything, much as they did in 2000 when the Mets and Yankees hooked up for a classic World Series matchup. The winner didn't just play the next day; the winner won the brass, and the loser went fishing for the winter.

Game 1 in the '55 Series played out in the Bronx, and the Yankees edged us out 6–5. The matchup was a classic one—Don Newcombe versus Whitey Ford. The best in the game stared the lineups down for what seemed a fifteen-round heavyweight fight. We traded punches back and forth, and they emerged the winners.

The Yankees took Game 2 as well at Yankee Stadium, and when the scene shifted to Ebbets Field, it was crisis time—do or die.

At Ebbets Field, Jackie Robinson takes a warm-up swing from his trademark pigeon-toed stance. The signature is authentic.

The Ebbets Field batting cage and the Boys of Summer: Reese, Furillo, Robinson, Erskine, Hodges, Newcombe, Snider, and Campanella *Courtesy of Ozzie Sweet*

My childhood buddies Johnny Wilson (center) and high school catcher Jack Rector (right).

Jackie with Branch Rickey, the Dodgers owner who signed him and instructed him to "turn the other cheek"

Leaving the field with Campy after striking out a then-record fourteen New York Yankees in a 3–2 victory in Game 3 of the 1953 World Series
Bettmann/CORBIS

I get a victory kiss from Betty after winning Game 3 of the 1953 Series. *Bettmann/CORBIS*

Serving food to American GIs at Ebbets Field on Armed Forces Day, August 30, 1953: (left to right) Clem Labine, a younger Carl Erskine, Jackie Robinson, and Preacher Roe *National Baseball Hall of Fame Library, Cooperstown, New York*

Opening day batting order, 1954: (left to right) Jim Gilliam, Pee Wee Reese, Duke Snider, Jackie Robinson, Manager Walter Alston, Roy Campanella, Gil Hodges, Carl Furillo, Billy Cox, and me

Six Dodgers were selected for the 1954 National League All-Star Team: (left to right) Manager Walter Alston, me, Jackie Robinson, Pee Wee Reese, Roy Campanella, Duke Snider, and Gil Hodges.

Robinson puts on the brakes rounding third. *Courtesy of Sal Larocca*

Campy and I go over the hitters in Roosevelt Stadium, Jersey City. Walter O'Malley scheduled a few games here trying to stay in the New York area.

TOP TO BOTTOM
PUDDIN' HEAD JONES
JACKIE ROBINSON
ANDY SEMINICK
GRANNY HAMNER
RUSS MEYER
EDDY WAITKUS
CHARLIE DRESSEN

Jackie was so quick he nearly always got out of a rundown. He actually scored on this play against the Phillies. *Courtesy of the Los Angeles Dodgers*

Old friend and battery mate Roy Campanella, paralyzed and confined to a wheelchair following an automobile accident, watches me warm up during a spring training session, 1959. Roy caught me in more than a thousand innings.
UPI Telephoto

With Campy watching from his hospital bed in New York, I was inspired to pitch my last complete game, in May 1958, a 2–1 win over the Phillies. Don Zimmer (right) knocked in the winning run.

A crowd of 80,000 watches the first pitch of first game ever played at the Los Angeles Coliseum, April 18, 1958. With Clem Labine's help I picked up the win against the Giants. *United Press Telephoto*

A pitch I didn't want to throw: the wrecking ball for the demolition of Ebbets Field in 1960.

(Left to right) Jackie, me, Dale W. McMillen, Bob Feller, and Ted Williams at a baseball clinic for Wildcat kids in Fort Wayne, Indiana *Courtesy of Wildcat Baseball*

Speaking to 5,000 Wildcat kids in Ft. Wayne, Indiana, 1961. Jackie often accompanied me to a variety of youth events.

Rachel and Mr. McMillen at a Wildcat awards banquet

Jackie, Duke, and me in an early-1970s appearance on "Sports Challenge," taped at Los Angeles TV station KTLA. Jackie has just answered a question correctly for host Dick Enberg.

Jimmy and I share a spot on the Dodgers bench at a Dodgertown training camp; he wants to bat.

Game 3 was pivotal for us on two levels—the mathematical level that no team had come back from a 3–0 deficit to win a World Series and the emotional level of being down once more to our archrivals. We needed to come away with a victory if we were going to give our fans and ourselves, for that matter, any real hopes of winning the Series. Players, contrary to popular belief, feel the emotional turbulence of a crucial loss just as the fan in the stands does. Only we choose not to always voice our exasperation in public because it neither changes the facts nor benefits the team psyche.

Johnny Podres was brilliant on the mound in Game 3 and kept the Yankees at bay the entire game. The only challenge was to score some runs for Johnny, which we did early on. The Yanks scored two runs in the second inning and one in the seventh, and that was it. Johnny pitched a complete game for us and got us a much-needed win, 8–3. Roy Campanella hit a crucial home run to ensure the victory. But as Yogi is often quoted as saying, "It ain't over till it's over." The Yankees just had that aura to them that they could win whenever they needed to, and we did as well in the National League, but they were the top guns.

My buddy Clem Labine got the win in Game 4, another key game because we needed to tie up the Series. Roy Campanella, Duke Snider, and Gil Hodges hit big home runs for us for the runaway victory in the fourth and fifth innings, when we scored three runs in each inning.

Game 5 saw us beat the Yankees once again, by a score of 5–3. Bob Cerv and Yogi Berra crushed long ones for the Yanks and we countered with blasts from Sandy and Duke. Rookie Roger Craig, the youngster on the team, got the win, and I was glad for him. He had worked hard to get to the big leagues and proved himself in the postseason.

Now the pressure was finally on *them*. *They* were the ones down 3–2 in games. *They* needed to win a game to stave off elimination.

Game 6 was a classic Yankees comeback in which they promptly scored five runs in the first inning to the delight of the Yankee Stadium faithful, and they won the game by the score of 5–1.

This was the moment we had all waited for—the decisive seventh game. It had been three years since a Game 7 decided it all. Johnny Podres took the mound and stayed there until the celebration was on—a complete-game eight-hit shutout. There were no home runs, no fanfare. It was just good old-fashioned commonsense baseball—a pitchers' duel with defensive gems. To celebrate a championship was wonderful, but to do it in front of more than sixty thousand Yankees fans *at* Yankee Stadium made the victory all the sweeter.

Brooklyn had finally done it. We as a borough had stamped our franchise as a dynasty. We had made it to three World Series in only four years!

Jackie, I know, felt that this one was special, and he knew that one day there would be volumes written about this 1955 World Series and our storied team. Even now, fifty years later, the men who remain from that club get a disproportionate amount of fan mail compared to our personal achievements. We are all reminded on an almost daily basis of the joy of playing in Brooklyn.

The fans had an identification with us that was beyond baseball. It was a societal identification that was parallel to Jackie's struggle. The Brooklyn fan wanted to be a Dodgers fan because he wanted to tell the world that he was a fan of Jackie's team. He wanted to tell everyone that he was a fan of a collection of men who were from all walks of life and represented the little guy trying to get ahead. The victory was multifaceted and was felt throughout the entire city.

After all, this was the team with the Sym-Phony Band and Gladys Gooding, the famed organist who knew everyone's hometown song and played it for them for each at bat. Instead of getting into the batter's box for spun clips of Springsteen, Bon Jovi,

Sting, or P. Diddy as players do today, we heard "Carolina Moon," "My Old Kentucky Home," and "Back Home in Indiana." The Sym-Phony band, with Jo Jo and Brother Lou, did so many oompahs to the opposing players when they struck out that they could have filled an entire CD if such a thing had existed. The American Federation of Music actually complained to Walter O'Malley that the "band" was "nonunion." I'm sure they felt honored to even be called a band. They were a collection of wiseacres with instruments. They did this for fun when they weren't running around the subway terminals. They finally settled with the union. Thank God for that, or we might have lost our band. We loved them as part of our extended family. They were our friends.

We had Hilda Chester, who was the First Lady of fans. She was the leather-lunged woman whom you could hear from the rafters. She had once yelled, "Branca! Branca! Look at me when I talk to you!" She was the same woman who once handed Pete Reiser a note to give to Leo Durocher, to which Pete obliged. The note asked Leo to put Hugh Casey in the game. Leo inserted Hugh Casey, and the Dodgers lost.

"You tell that S.O.B. MacPhail never to give me a note again!" Leo yelled at Reiser after the loss. Durocher was at his best—and funniest—when he was angry.

Pete explained to Leo that the note wasn't from team president Larry MacPhail, but from Hilda—and he just passed it along! Only in Brooklyn!

These were the same fans who bid Willie Mays a fond farewell by slashing his tires in the parking lot early in Mays's career after the all-star homered twice in one game off us. Mays told Durocher, who at that point was managing the Giants, that he wanted to be escorted from the park the next time out.

Finally, after many years of waiting, the fans were able to taste the good life of being champions. In fact, a group of real cult fans make a public ritual of visiting the Ebbets Field site, even to this day, every October 4 at 3:43 p.m., the exact date and time when Pee Wee threw to Hodges at first to get Elston Howard and win it all for Brooklyn.

Nobody knew it at the time, but this was the beginning of the end for all of us as we knew each other. The only separation that lay between where we were, at the height of popularity, and leaving Brooklyn and disbanding the team was one single season— 1956. This was the last year of any joy in Brooklyn, and all season long it was marred by bitter battles between Walter O'Malley and the city of New York.

It's ironic that the critics of the game desire that their icons retire gracefully, and yet ownership never moves a franchise gracefully, never negotiates with a city gracefully. The same critics wanted Jackie to take the ribbing gracefully, which he did for an ungodly number of years, and yet O'Malley and Robert Moses couldn't keep their animosity to themselves, and both were well-to-do businessmen who were doing what they loved in life without any pressure from society. The cruel blade of irony once again made incisions in our pastime and in our hearts forever.

Moses got his way by chasing not one, but two, major-league teams out of New York. The only consolation for New Yorkers was the Mets, a 1962 expansion team. I think it's a weak apology to the fans that the Mets' team colors are the Dodgers' blue and the Giants' orange.

9
Mr. Intensity—1956

I OFTEN THOUGHT OF JACKIE ROBINSON as "Mr. Intensity." He had a fire within him. He was intent on being intense about baseball. His desire to realize team accolades and to be the best player in the National League was unparalleled. Jackie saw the urgency to go back to the World Series this year, and that tenacity reared its glorious and beautiful head in an early May baseball game against our archrival Giants.

What made Jackie skip a category from a great player to a legendary player, in my book, was his ability to transfer that emotional energy into the clubhouse and into the minds of the men around him.

Jackie was one of those rare athletes who had the ability to make those of us around him better athletes. Jackie could have been a great manager. I really admired him for this aspect of his personality, and I know it affected my life in an extremely positive way. It was something I took with me when I left baseball and went into coaching.

It takes only seconds to reflect on one particular day when Jackie's fire helped me achieve baseball immortality—if only for one game. I spoke about this moment at the 1997 ESPY Awards in New York City. It was the fiftieth anniversary of Jackie's debut for the Dodgers and breaking barriers. The director of the ESPYs asked me to recount an incident that illustrated Jackie's competitive spirit, and I couldn't think of a better story than that of my second no-hitter.

It was May 12, 1956, an otherwise nondescript day, unless you count the Giants' and Dodgers' hatred for each other down to the core of our woolen jerseys. It was a hot Saturday morning; but however scorching it was in Central Park, there was an inferno moving southward from Connecticut to Brooklyn—the one inside Jackie's belly.

"The Dodgers are over the hill. Jackie's too old. Campy's too old, and Erskine couldn't win another game with the garbage that he's throwing up there. . . ." So went the newspaper clipping quoting Giants chief scout Tom Sheehan that Saturday morning in the tabloids. Apparently, Tom wasn't concerned about making astute assessments.

I was scheduled to pitch that afternoon, and, as the papers implied, I was having a bit of arm trouble and was mired in my own pitching slump, if you want to label it that.

Not wanting to miss my start, I took the warm-up ball from Walter. I had taken a cortisone shot, but nobody knew about it. After finishing warm-ups, I took the mound, just praying for some easy innings at the beginning. Any pitcher who's having arm trouble prays for some easy outs early on because it takes about two innings to get in a good groove. That's why great pitchers are either lit up early or end up winning the game. Whether it was Sal Maglie or Don Newcombe in our day or Randy Johnson, Roger Clemens, or Pedro Martinez in the modern era, if you didn't get to these men early, you didn't get to them at all.

My personal prayer was readily answered.

The first three innings went as smooth as butter. A few grounders, some easy fly balls, and I was sailing along past the third inning. The fourth inning also went well, but, unfortunately for me, Al Worthington of the Giants was pitching lights-out as well.

I just knew this was going to be a long spring day at the ballpark if I was to notch a win for myself.

It was a classic duel on the mound—and between two rival New York teams who fiercely hated each other.

The fifth inning reared its ugly head too soon for me. The fifth inning is often the crucial one because the game becomes official after five innings and the flow of a game can change on a dime sometimes.

I threw Willie Mays a low inside fastball, and he ripped a bullet off the ground to Jackie's left at third base. In the flash of an eye, Jackie scooped it up and threw in what looked like one fluid motion. The throw beat the speedy Mays at first base, and all was well. I knew, right then and there, as I stood by the mound watching the split-second events happen, that this would be the play of the game. All no-hitters have one great play. It's mathematics. You can't pitch a no-hitter on pure pitching skill. Only Jackie could have made that play. He had the agility and instincts, knowing how to fire the ball to first after the pivot to beat out Mays.

We finally scored three in the seventh. I had no close calls in the eighth inning. So it all came down to one inning—three outs to go. Up until this point I hadn't dwelled on the fact that I hadn't allowed any hits. This type of thinking and anticipation can kill a pitcher's ego and ruin a no-hit bid. In a situation like mine, the only thing I was thinking was one pitch, one batter at a time. A leather-lunged Brooklyn fan kept informing me, "Hey, Oisk, you got a no-hitter going!"

In the ninth inning I was able to get two quick outs. And then Alvin Dark strode to the batter's box. He made me nervous. He made all of the National League pitchers nervous. He was a contact hitter, which is a disaster for anyone trying to end a no-hitter, because he almost always made contact with the ball, and where there's contact, there's usually a hole in the diamond through which the ball can find its way.

I made what I thought was a perfect pitch to Alvin, my over-hand curve, and he hit a one-hopper back to the mound. Hodges, at first, made me take my time. I fielded it and threw to first.

I now had the second no-hitter of my career. Jackie rushed in to congratulate me—the first one in! Campy came simultaneously to the mound to hug me, and Pee Wee and the other guys poured in from all directions. Then we noticed that Jackie had turned and was headed toward the third-base line.

Approaching the area where Tom Sheehan was sitting, Jackie stopped, reached into his back pocket, and produced the news-paper clipping from that Saturday's paper with Tom Sheehan's quote in it and proceeded to wave it at Tom Sheehan and the entire Giants bench!

"How do you like that garbage!" Jackie yelled at the Giants' dugout, racing off as he yelled to rejoin our celebration.

Clem Labine later recalled to me how Jackie had doubled in the tenth inning to win a game for him in the 1956 World Series against the Yankees—this was nine years after Jackie's debut—and a photo of the two of them appeared in the paper. Clem said he received a piece of hate mail from a fan who said, "How can you play with him?"

I know that Jim Gilliam benefited from Jackie's tutelage. Jim looked up to Jackie. He idolized Jackie, and for good reason. Jackie taught him that to get mad was self-defeating. "Do as I say and not as I do" was the attitude Robinson tried to convey to Jim, because he didn't want Jim to have a tenuous reputation with the press. This was just another aspect of Jackie that amazed me—the will and the desire to be a mentor. Mentoring is not something that a player wakes up one morning and does. It is a desire that must come from within him and must be the product of an unselfish personality.

Once when we were playing the Giants, Sal Maglie, "the Bar-ber," threw me a knockdown pitch, by accident. Maglie was known for flipping a few in his day—Pee Wee, Jackie, Furillo. He had a well-deserved reputation as a headhunter; he was the only person who never smiled or uttered a word when he passed you by in the tunnels leading to the clubhouses. He prided himself on this type of mental and physical intimidation.

The Dodgers' bench raced to my defense, with Jackie leading the cause: "The ball hit him! He got hit!"

Jocko Conlon turned to me. "All right. Carl, did you get hit?" he asked me.

I was in such a stupor that the only thing I could think about was that I was OK. Nothing seemed broken, and I didn't remember any contact by the ball because I fell flat on my back too fast to remember anything. I told the truth.

"Jocko, I don't think so. I think it hit the knob of the bat," I said.

Jackie looked at me and asked, "How could you do that after I defended you?"

Sorry, pal. This was a moment of profound stupor on my part. I was too shaken up by the incident to say anything but what I thought happened out there in those few seconds.

Today, the closest brouhaha of that sort came from the Roger Clemens–Mike Piazza incident in the summer of 2000, and then again in the World Series in that year, the first Subway Series since the one in which I was involved in 1956.

Watching Mike Piazza go down like he did that summer sent chills down my spine. I admire Roger Clemens and what he has done for the game—and I don't think he meant to hurt Mike—but I can only imagine what it was like for Mike Piazza to be lying there dazed and scared.

It is impossible for a fan or anyone who hasn't played the game to imagine the split-second reflexes necessary to dodge a fastball tailing inside. The body just can't react that quickly. Fear takes over. Mental paralysis sets in, and then you have the ultimate tragedy.

Baseball has not been a stranger to severe incidents involving hit batters, but the situations can be decreased drastically by eliminating a desire to want to go head-hunting.

The drama that surrounded Clemens and Piazza's next encounter, in the 2000 World Series, really shocked me. I saw a shattered bat, the shattered end hurled in Piazza's direction, and then some words exchanged.

Clemens claimed he was reacting to the splintered edge. Piazza claimed it was hurled at him. Whatever the outcome, the situation was tenuous, and it provoked faulty recollections on the part of fellow baseball players.

"None of that happened in my day" was the dialogue uttered by some of my comrades in baseball arms. Not true.

I vehemently disagreed with them.

Leo Durocher and Charlie Dressen used to have a philosophy of baseball that is as dangerous today as it was then—the give-'em-two-for-one rule.

"If they—the opposition—knock down one of our guys, we'll give 'em two for one!" Leo used to say to us in the locker room.

"If one of ours goes down, two of theirs will go down!" Dressen would admonish our starting staff.

This accelerated the beanball incidents and only helped to portray the game as thuggish.

A player's heart is his den of inner solace. Only he knows his thought processes out there on the mound and the intent, or lack thereof, behind an inside pitch that knocks a batter flat.

However, there is a difference between a manager logically instructing a pitcher to pitch inside, so as to move a hitter off the plate, versus explicitly directing that pitcher to intentionally throw at a player's head. The latter should be better restricted.

Batters lose respect for pitchers who throw at them rather than move them off the plate. Randy Johnson can move hitters off the plate. Don Drysdale had an exceptionally low delivery and release point, making his fastball run in on hitters, but Drysdale had a presence of mind.

"I'm taking half the plate, and I'm giving the hitter half the plate; that's fair, right?" he'd say.

"Only I'm not telling them which half!" Drysdale would quip.

He'd run a fastball inside on a hitter, and he'd stick his chin out as if to say, "I meant it," even though his control might have been off that day. And so he was dubbed a headhunter. Don, however, was a pure professional. If he had to protect one of his teammates, he'd do it in the bat of an eyelash without so much as an uttered word. He wasn't a brash talker like some. He didn't ever say, "I'm going to get him" or anything of the kind. He was above those kinds of remarks.

His body language after the pitch was thrown intimated the unspoken words, and I always believed that was an act in itself.

In my era, if a hitter bunted on a pitcher, the manly thing to do was wing him next time he came to the plate.

"Nothing but blue sky he'll be seeing, bunting on me," was the macho response of the day.

To me, all this did was expose the pitcher's weaknesses and show he lacked composure under pressure.

You have to have the right personality to throw knockdowns and make them fairly effective. It wasn't in my cards. I didn't have the personality to do it, and on the few occasions I did I was less than effective.

I always felt that intimidation through brains, not brawn, worked a heck of a lot better. Jackie Robinson was an expert in this area.

When we visited the Milwaukee Braves in '56, the first East Coast team to head West, Jackie, who in those days was given a day off at times, used to stand around the infield during batting practice while the Braves were hitting and tell them, "I'm playing today!"

As I stood around the warm-up area near the batting cage, I saw firsthand the psychological paralysis setting in: guys would swing at bad pitches during the game to force something to happen.

I admired this type of intensity. I thrived on it; we all did. Jackie's intensity took me back to my own intensity for winning and to thoughts of my friend Johnny Wilson.

My channel for my anguish was my music. My Midwestern, Anderson, Indiana, roots taught me well about starry nights, open farmland, and playing the harmonica. That harmonica came in handy after one particularly heartbreaking loss in St. Louis.

I was beaten by Stan Musial in St. Louis, 2–1, on a walk-off home run in the ninth inning by "the Man" with only one out to go—something a pitcher never forgets.

The train ride to Chicago was a listless one, and so I attempted to channel the sorrow, and anger, into some musical lamentation.

I called the song "The Stan Musial Blues." It had no lyrics but lots of pain and suffering, as well as a full array of octave-changing, blues-style, syncopated schemes.

Expression through music for me was peaceful and productive. I often wondered how I'd handle what Jackie had to go through—and I couldn't come up with a song for that situation. Jackie was once again swimming upstream, and all we could do was lifeguard the waters. But both Jackie and my grade-school pal Johnny Wilson, though different in personality, could have played in any era because of their tenacity.

I learned by observing both men—and when you sit back and just watch somebody, the impact can be such that it takes your own game to the next level.

Don Newcombe was another guy in the big leagues who learned volumes from Jackie, but there was something about Don that I didn't learn until well after it was out in the open in the press.

It's amazing that an athlete can be a teammate for years, and some facets of his life remain a mystery. Some guys didn't let us in on their personal problems. Such was the case with Don New-combe and Don's problem with alcohol. When we toured Japan, we all knew that Newk took in a few beers, but that was the end of it, or so we thought.

He was deathly afraid of flying, and he always took a bottle of scotch with him on the plane to help keep him loose. Still, we thought it was no big deal. Alcohol is a problem that gradually sneaks up on a person. We never knew Don not to be in peak condition before a start throughout his career.

I knew Don as a strikeout king, a Rookie of the Year, an MVP, a Cy Young Award winner, and a great guy on and off the field, but I never found out about his alcohol problem until years later.

Don's relationship with the press grew tenuous in '56, the beginning of the slide with the media. They thought he was belligerent to begin with—I thought he was misunderstood by them. He was an early African-American ballplayer with a lot on his plate to cope with, and I thought that the press misunderstood his comments.

Newk's stats, in the opinion of everyone who ever played with him, make him a solid Hall of Fame candidate. He was one of our greatest players by the close of the '56 season, earning twenty-seven wins and ending the year with a Herculean .794 winning percentage. How many pitchers in history have accomplished that feat? Not many. The writers put their personal opinions ahead of good baseball sense by not electing Don to the Baseball Hall of Fame.

However, as history has shown us before, outspokenness has its price, and it had its price on this superstar.

Jackie Robinson, at the end of the 1956 season, found himself outside of Walter O'Malley's coveted group of insiders.

O'Malley disliked Rickey and Rickey's men. Yet, throughout the purge of the Rickey Dodgers executives and perimeter players and managers, he kept that critical core nucleus intact.

Jackie Robinson, in Walter's mind, represented the Branch Rickey era, and, still bitter—six years after the fact—about the way

O'Malley perceived Rickey's handling of the sale of the team and the transfer of power to him, O'Malley decided that Jackie would always be a Rickey disciple. He was either for Walter or against him. It came down to the hardest of hard-line stances. O'Malley was bothered by Jackie's outspokenness and his controversial newspaper column.

"If I ever get traded and it's not to a New York team, I'll quit," Jackie made clear in the papers when the brouhaha started.

I didn't want to leave this world without knowing why the Dodgers would ever consider trading their greatest player in history. So in later years at a benefit, I asked Buzzy Bavasi, the general manager, why they traded Jackie. Buzzy knew I demanded an immediate, and honest, answer, and so he looked me straight in the eye and without any hesitation told me that Walter wanted to get rid of him.

"I'm sick of him popping off and his outbursts. Get rid of him!"

So went the immortal words of Walter O'Malley to his general manager Buzzy Bavasi that fateful day in 1956 when Dodgers fans learned that Jackie Robinson had been traded to the accursed Giants. It was as if the fans had been robbed and then kicked while they were down. First they lost Robinson, and then later they lost their team.

Jackie, true to his character and his sense of team loyalty, refused the trade and subsequently retired, ending a brilliant but all-too-short career in baseball.

Ironically, the Dodgers crumbled soon afterward, almost as punishment from the heavens for the embarrassing final days of Jackie Robinson's tenure as a Dodger.

10

The Future Is Not
What It Used to Be

I ONCE READ AN OLD church sign that said, "The trouble with today is the future is not what it used to be."

The 1957 season marked the official home stretch for the Brooklyn Dodgers and New York Giants as New York knew them. After this season it would be so long, Brooklyn, and hello, Los Angeles.

Although the New York Giants signed with San Francisco city officials to officially move the franchise before we did, Walter O'Malley had the idea of coast-to-coast baseball in the back of his mind ever since the jet age began.

The Dodgers were the first team to use airplanes to travel within the state of Florida for spring-training games. No other club used prop planes of any sort. It was a harbinger of the technology to come for America post-Korea. The move to Los Angeles, contrary to what has been written, had nothing to do with the Braves bolting out of Boston in 1953 and heading west to Milwaukee. It had, however, everything to do with the jet age. Technology drove baseball because O'Malley was fascinated by it. He loved planes and used a DC-3 in spring training. We had our own pilot—Bump Holman. O'Malley loved the idea that he could be in L.A. from Vero Beach in just five and a half hours.

The fights between Robert Moses, the chief administrator of the Federal Housing Association, and Walter O'Malley had taken their toll on the city. Moses wanted roads. O'Malley wanted a new stadium at the corner of Atlantic and Flatbush Avenues at the old Long Island Railroad (LIRR) terminal.

Walter was a born-and-bred New Yorker. He knew nothing about the West Coast. Moses refused to compromise. He was a man who had to have his way. He wanted highways and a multi-purpose facility on the Flushing Meadows grounds—where the Arthur Ashe Tennis Center and Shea Stadium now reside. Walter thought that forty thousand people could be moved within a half hour on the LIRR and that the money everyone saved on parking would be spent on concessions. He also wanted a base-ball-only facility. In desperation, Walter had us play regular-season games at Roosevelt Stadium in Jersey City, New Jersey, against the Braves and Reds.

I won a couple of games at Roosevelt Stadium. To prove his point that he needed a new ballpark and would try to keep the Dodgers in the tristate area, O'Malley went to these great lengths. But why didn't Walter go to Flushing Meadows? The answer is unclear, but it rests within the irreparable rift between Moses and O'Malley.

Moses was not about to let O'Malley thwart his plans for a road right through Williamsburg—the Brooklyn-Queens Expressway.

O'Malley looked out his window at Montague Street and said he saw unemployment lines growing and season-ticket holders turning in tickets. Walter was convinced that the status quo just could not continue. Something, or someone, had to give.

As for Jackie, he had predicted that the disenfranchisement of African Americans would haunt the nation because America couldn't keep denying bright young men jobs and expect every-thing to work itself out in the end. Even New York, ahead of most states in civil rights, was not fully prepared to afford African Americans adequate employment opportunities. Walter O'Malley was caught in the middle and, deciding it wasn't worth the fight anymore with the Housing Administration, decided to bolt to Los Angeles for an offer he couldn't refuse: three hundred acres of undeveloped property in downtown Los Angeles. He didn't get the LIRR terminal, but he did get a gift location at the apex of the L.A. freeway system.

There was a buy-sell agreement in Branch Rickey's contract that allowed him as a minority stockholder to sell his stock, but first he had to offer it back to the current stockholders in the event of a sale of the stock. So Walter thought back then all would work out fine. If another bidder entered the picture, O'Malley had to meet it. Rickey went to a friend of his, William Zeckendorf, who was the Donald Trump of the 1950s in New York, and as a Realtor he had no problem putting the heat on O'Malley. O'Malley felt the offer was a trumped-up deal to jack up the price. He matched the offer and paid the extra fee to Zeckendorf, namely his commission. The friction caused by that never went away in the head of O'Malley.

It made O'Malley detest Rickey, and it made O'Malley intolerant of another Rickey situation—as was the case with Robert Moses. It is unfortunate that two of the greatest baseball minds— O'Malley and Rickey—couldn't get together on a deal. I saw the architect's model of the domed stadium idea in 1955—the one Buckminster Fuller wanted to build at Atlantic and the LIRR terminal. The model was light-years ahead of its time, years ahead of the Astrodome, which became famous and which has since been abandoned for Minute Maid Park in Houston.

"Carl, this stadium will be temperature-controlled and will be atmospherically right for baseball," Walter told me.

"And someday cities will exist like this! New York City could be in a situation where we have controlled climates," he added. He was way out in some respects, but he was serious. His domed stadium idea took off, and now there are retractable domed stadiums identical to Walter's in Arizona, Seattle, and Toronto. Unfortunately, Walter didn't fight hard enough to see his idea come to fruition. Brooklyn was an orphan borough—a borough without political clout. It was a "City of Churches." It had botanical gardens and lots of culture but in many ways was the forgotten borough. Only in Brooklyn could neighborhoods have a highway —the BQE—built right through their heart. In the end, Roz Wyman and Southern California won out. She became the talk of the nation as the young congresswoman who had snagged the Dodgers away from Brooklyn, with the help of the mayor of Los Angeles, and Brooklyn became just plain heartbroken.

The players were kept out of the loop throughout all of these events. So my job as player rep, while all of these bitter paper wars were waging, was to convince Major League Baseball to contribute more money to our disgraceful pension plan. Our pension was a token—in name only. As of 1950, players had to play five years to get any benefit at age sixty-five, and that was fifty dollars per month. Each extra year you played, you received ten dollars more per month. If you played ten years, you could get one hundred per month, and that was the maximum. In many cases players didn't complete the critical fifth year to be eligible for the pension.

Most of the time we negotiated with the owners for menial details, such as not playing night games on getaway days so we wouldn't have to ride the train all night to play the next afternoon.

Our first big win in the boardroom came in 1950, which by 1957 seemed a lifetime behind us, when Happy Chandler sold the rights to the World Series and All-Star Games to network television, the first-ever sale of this sort. Chandler received six million dollars for the rights for five years. The players hired J. Norman Lewis as a negotiator guide, and we took the lead from Commissioner Chandler, who declared, "There are clubs in this league that will never fund a pension because they're not making money."

He was right. The Browns were always claiming loss of revenue. The Senators lost money as well. The television deal introduced new money into their budgets, and so we approached the owners and negotiated directly for the allotment of this cash to our pension plan. The owners agreed to a 60-40 split of the new money, with the players getting 60 percent. As the fifties rolled along, the television sets sold themselves and the contracts ballooned up. The owners finally had to tell the players that they couldn't give the same 60 percent as usual. (The same contract, now including playoffs and World Series games, in its most recent negotiation with Fox, went for more than a billion dollars.) In 1957, the owners decided to put a flat amount into the pension each year. Ralph Kiner and Allie Reynolds were the spokesmen for the NL and AL, respectively, and were keys to the success of the players' pension plan.

There was one big team moment. It came in the form of a big brouhaha that defined the year that ironically had us break hearts. It reminded us of the tenacity of Jackie Robinson, even though he was no longer in uniform. His soul was echoed through Jackie's protégé, Jim Gilliam.

Nineteen fifty-seven was our first year in Brooklyn without Jackie and our last year there as a team. It was ironic and bittersweet—as it should have been because moving was no fun. We wanted to stay in Brooklyn, not head West.

But Jim made Jackie proud in '57 with a drag bunt in a game against Cincinnati that summer. It just went to prove that whenever a pitcher headhunts, it can come back to haunt him. The man on the mound in that game was a pitcher named Raul Sanchez.

Sanchez became a folkloric part of our last year in Brooklyn. Raul played in the big leagues for only three short seasons, but he made quite an impact on our club while pitching for the Reds in 1957.

His duties on the Reds were more as a middle reliever, by today's terminology. He'd be called into the game in about the sixth inning to hold the opposing team and try to keep the Reds in the game.

However, he quickly established a reputation for hitting two or three guys in the inning in which he was due to be lifted for a pinch hitter. At least that was the way it appeared. One particular night at Crosley Field that summer, he drilled our friend, Jim Gilliam, right in the ribs. It was indisputable that the drilling was intentional. Everyone knew it was because the ball landed right where he wanted it to, but Jim didn't charge the mound. Instead, he remembered Jackie's philosophy about keeping your mouth shut and letting your playing speak for you. Jackie's credo lived on while his uniform number 42 lay folded away in the Dodgers' clubhouse.

Jim simply walked to first base, without so much as exchanging a word, and took his HBP. There was no brouhaha, and the game ended with a Dodgers victory. Jim told me that nothing needed to be said. The Reds were due back in town in just a few weeks. He said he'd be ready. We knew we'd be ready.

Several weeks went by, and the Reds came to town. For most of us, the incident in Cincinnati was long forgotten, but not to Jim. In the middle of the game, Sanchez was called in to face Gilliam. Once again the tension mounted. Only this time, Jim took that bat back, and as the pitch came in, he squared away.

Jim dragged a bunt down the first-base line with the precision of an artist painting a rolling ball on a piece of canvas. It wasn't unusual for Gilliam to lay down a bunt like that. Sanchez came over to field the ball, and Jim hit him like an eighteen-wheeler roaring down I-95! Once Sanchez was on the ground, Jim pounded the living daylights out of him.

The benches emptied. We raced in. They raced in. All of a sudden I saw Don Hoak coming toward Jim, like a madman. Don's nickname was "Tiger." He hailed from Roulette, Pennsylvania, was a former marine, and was proud of it in every way.

Charlie Neal, who stood about two inches shorter than Hoak and hailed from Longview, Texas, saw Hoak's eyes affixed on Jim. As Hoak raced toward Jim, Neal raced toward Hoak.

At the very moment when Hoak attempted to land a haymaker, Charlie Neal connected on Hoak's chin with a punch that would have devastated any heavyweight boxing champion. I have never seen, in all my years watching boxing matches, a punch landed with such force, and so uncontested because of the element of surprise. Hoak was sent reeling backward, causing him to fall flat over the pitcher's mound. And Charlie Neal was the new heavyweight champ.

Gilliam had made his point—Jackie Robinson must have been proud.

The end was approaching, faster than we wanted. It was September, and there was one final chapter that had to be written. As with the death of any loved one, before the transportation to a final resting place, there must be a funeral and a eulogy.

We had our own funeral for our beloved Brooklyn Dodgers and old Ebbets Field in our heart of hearts that last day—September 24, 1957. It was short. It wasn't sweet but rather extremely bitter, and we didn't stay around for the final remarks.

"Please do not go on the field, and use the nearest exit to Chavez Ravine," Tex Rickard, the public-address announcer, told the fans for us at the end of the game.

Gladys Gooding played "May the Good Lord Bless and Keep You."

Duke Snider remarked that he "didn't want to play that last game."

We all felt that way. It was embarrassing to go out on the field and say good-bye to our beloved fans. Jackie would have felt the same way—and here was a man who retired rather than play for any other team, so his allegiance to Brooklyn was unquestionable.

I thought about the good old days when we were all together. I thought about the first spring-training days—the days of wine and roses. The days of all of our kids—Snider, Campy, Duke, Preacher Roe, and Rube Walker—playing together were fading. The days of Morris Steiner, the pediatrician in the neighborhood, taking care of our kids were fading as well. We were leaving Joe Rossi's Butcher Shop, and Bob and Roz Baumann, who ran a day camp in Oceanside, Long Island, and would send a van for the Dodgers' kids every day.

As young players we wanted to bring our wives to spring training, but we didn't have the money to rent or lease a house. Wives, in the early years, were not permitted at the Dodgertown training camp, and so Duke and I shared a house—Betty and Bev alternated cooking the evening meals. Our families grew. We grew together as one big tree, with each of us adding a branch, whether it was a daughter or a son. Suddenly I had two sons, and Duke had a son and a daughter. This housing arrangement went on for several years. There was never a tense moment. There were no strained relations or breaches in our relationship as teammates. We were one big Dodgers family.

We were all little kids in grown bodies and still wanted to go out and play together like old times. But time has a way of making sure the playgrounds are swept clean for the next generation. A finite amount of time is awarded us to play in the dirt and leave our tracks. Then the time comes when we must all come inside from recess and clean up. This was cleanup time for us older Dodgers players.

Although Dodgertown was physically the same as it had been in 1948, the life was missing from the air. The old routine of heading North was gone. The old routine of Campy, Furillo, and I going fishing was gone. No more Preacher Roe bass fishing after practice in air boats. Jackie was not playing anymore. I walked out onto the field and remembered the old times when we left Dodgertown in late March and headed North, usually playing our way through Jacksonville, New Orleans, Atlanta, Nashville (usually against the Braves), and so forth.

Not this year. In 1958, in spring training, we knew when we boarded that DC jet that we were heading out to California not just for a new season but to make new lives for ourselves. Instead of seeing tiny dots representing Myrtle Beach and Washington, D.C., we were getting glimpses of the Rocky Mountains, with a lifetime of memories left behind. A dramatic change of course was in store for us, as Los Angeles was different from Brooklyn in every conceivable regard. From that point on, our careers would never be the same.

"It was as if we had left our second home," Clem reflected.

An entire era was now closed, with a new one beginning. We had said hello to each other just a decade before this trip West, and now it was time to say good-bye, New York, and hello, Los Angeles.

It felt like school days—those dreaded days in September when the butterflies run rampant because a new year, a new grade has come, and with that new year new responsibilities.

Some of us—Don Newcombe, Pee Wee, Gil Hodges, Duke, Furillo, and yours truly—had already had our best years. We were now in the twilight of our careers. Now the anxiety of "can we do it again" was upon us.

But I had learned well from Jackie.

I had learned that life is all about making life better for the next generation, and so we all tried to impart our wisdom to the next generation of firebrands—Sandy Koufax and Don Drysdale.

Their outlook was quite different. Their future was about to happen. They were the new Los Angeles Dodgers in every way, shape, and form. Walter O'Malley gave Buzzy a $225,000 budget for both Koufax and Drysdale. Koufax wanted $125,000 and was promptly signed to that amount. Drysdale wanted his fair due and wanted $110,000, but Buzzy had only $100,000 left in the budget. Uneasy about the entire matter, Buzzy decided to go over budget and give Drysdale his $110,000. Walter didn't say a word to Buzzy. At the end of the season Walter sent Buzzy a note saying, "I hope Drysdale appreciated the extra $10,000 you gave him because that was your raise for next year."

Koufax and Drysdale were exactly what L.A. so desperately needed—two dependable young men whom fans could count on year in and year out. They were West Coast in every regard, even dress. When we coupled their tremendous pitching talents with the speed and hitting of Maury Wills, we had a great chance at some exciting games and a lot of potential W's on our scorecards.

11

My Pal, Campy

THERE WAS YET ANOTHER emotional impact, however, on our
plane trip to Los Angeles—the empty seat where our beloved
Campy should have been.

Roy and I were truly close buddies. He was my pal. We fished.
We did things together off the field. I truly loved him, and I rarely
use that word. There's a picture of the two of us embracing after
a no-hitter. I get teary every time I think of Roy. I can't help it—
he was so warm, so gentle.

In the old days, the team paired guys to room together so that
one could mentor the other. Campy roomed with Jackie briefly
and then roomed with rookie pitcher Don Newcombe. The
matchup was perfect because Campy soothed Newk, who was
young, talented, and brash.

Campy and Jackie saw eye to eye on everything; only their
methods differed. Campy admits to not being militant but "letting his bat do the talking." The press could never get their hands
on any divisions between the two, much as everyone kept pining
for them, because there weren't any divisions. The two loved and
respected one another. They just understood where each man differed. Both were right. Both were entitled to their own beliefs.

Campanella didn't win three MVP Awards just because he was
nice. He won them because he was the best catcher I ever saw.
He could field, hit for average, hit for power, and run. He had a
devastating throw to second to prevent guys from stealing off me.

Life was all smiles for us. A pitcher has a unique relationship with his catcher; that's why the term "battery mates" is used. A pitcher and catcher could be an island unto themselves during the course of a game. All the other positions become blocked out of a pitcher's mind, as in my case. The two of us thought alike, pitch by pitch. He gave the signs—I seldom shook him off—and I threw to him. We played catch for nine innings, day after day, year after year. I was officially "in" more than 350 games—spring training, exhibitions, World Series—and some 2,000 innings, and in most of them I was pitching to Roy.

I couldn't wait to see what Roy would do in the L.A. Coliseum and was excited that he was coming to California with me. I was looking to him to be a stabilizing force in this time of great emotional upheaval. Campy had schooled not only me; he was responsible for the successes of Joe Black and Don Newcombe, not to mention Clem Labine and the rest of our staff, including Preacher Roe.

I shot the film that is shown of Campy on his beloved boat, *The Princess*, named after his daughter. The eight-millimeter movies were taken in Long Island in Glen Cove, where Campy lived in J. P. Morgan's old estate. Campy and I fished off his boat but mainly fished in Vero Beach. Carl Furillo, Campy, and I fished off the Indian River in Florida, and when a fisherman fishes the Indian River, he's liable to catch anything. We caught sea trout and snook—a real fine game fish and fine eating fish. This wasn't really a river but rather the Atlantic Ocean running inside the island strips off the intercoastal waterway. Sharks, rays—both were caught at some point by us. We used bait-casting rods. Sometimes we used shrimp and live bait in salt water, and for fresh water we used artificial baits.

Walter Alston paid us the highest compliment as battery mates when he told the team, "When Campy and Erskine are battery mates I don't worry about the pitches." Walter knew how great a game caller Campy was, as did Dressen and Durocher, and they all respected and had professional love for this man. He had a sixth sense about calling pitches. In certain situations, with the game on the line, he would call for a pitch, usually a fastball right in the hitter's wheelhouse, that was the last place a hitter would ever expect a pitch. Strike three!

And then the news came—bit by bit—about as painful to hear as to see.

Roy was paralyzed from the neck down in a car accident on January 29, 1958. He was lying in a bed at Bellevue Hospital in New York and never got a chance to swing at that short 250-foot improvised left-field screen at Memorial Coliseum in L.A. I'll never forget the day I heard that news as long as I live. It had been a typical winter's night in New York. Cold, icy roads and late hours at Roy's off-season business led to tragedy. Roy had closed the liquor store that he owned late that night because he wanted the other workers to go home early. He took a fateful spin, and the crash sent him up-end. He knew when he couldn't move his body to turn the engine off in his car that he was paralyzed.

I learned about Roy's accident right after it happened—but strangely enough, from the man at the desk at the YMCA where I was working out.

"Did you hear about Campanella?" he asked me.

"No," I said.

"He was in a car accident," he informed me.

Few details, except the basic ones, followed as the news media was not then the mass television media we know of today.

There wasn't any Internet, cable television, or coast-to-coast news coverage on network television. News was mostly communicated via radio, newspaper, and on television only once at night—and briefly at that. I learned only that Roy was paralyzed from the neck down, and that killed me inside.

On our first road trip east I went to see Roy. I walked into that hospital room just as the family had left. I didn't know it beforehand, but I was the first visitor from the team, the hospital told me, and they allowed me to go inside. Before me, the doctor who had seen Roy had cried, seeing an idol of his lying there in that condition.

When I walked in and saw Roy stretched out like that I couldn't speak.

About five minutes went by and we said nothing. Tears welled up in our eyes. And then he broke the silence.

"Ersk, you got to get us a better medical plan. I had to have a tracheotomy—$8,500! I'm already wiped out." But then Roy became his old optimistic self.

"And tomorrow I go to therapy. I'm going to lift five pounds with my right hand," he said confidently and in an excited manner.

Chills went down my spine. I couldn't believe that this was the same man who had hit towering drives into the gas station beyond right field and had thrown out countless base runners with that right hand. Here he was, happy about going to therapy. It just showed me that courage came in all sorts of packages and with all sorts of outlooks. Roy was in a facedown position with a heavy neck brace. He said that with the aid of mirrors he'd be able to watch me pitch the next night.

I threw a complete-game two-hitter against the Phillies. It was the last complete game I ever pitched in my life. I knew Roy was watching—I could feel him on every pitch. I dedicated the win to him. Don Zimmer knocked in the winning run for me and forever earned a special spot in my heart, because I never wanted a personal win as badly as I wanted that one. I still hoped that one day Roy could walk once more and make a comeback.

I couldn't believe that the man with the smile as big as Long Island would spend the rest of his life in a wheelchair—thirty-three years and never a complaint. We held out hope that he could beat the paralysis and still hit those signature towering home runs of his, but those hopes never saw the light of day.

I don't think there was a dry eye in the park when Roy made it out of the hospital and out to L.A. for Roy Campanella Night. It was the largest crowd in baseball history—and remains so to this day. More than ninety-three thousand filled the old Los Angeles Coliseum to honor Roy. It was a benefit game between the Yankees and Dodgers to defray Roy's medical expenses, and I pitched.

The lights were dimmed; candles were lit. Dignitaries were on hand, and a ceremony followed. Everybody just let their emotions pour out. It was impossible to look at Roy and not be upset. This was a man who was incapable of harsh words, was incapable of hurting another human being, and was the best battery mate ever. He was the greatest catcher in baseball, to me, and his Hall of Fame status certainly makes that point.

I couldn't believe how Roy's life was turned upside down so quickly. There was nothing any of us could do to make life OK for him. And still, throughout the entire ordeal, Roy didn't have a bad thought in his head. He was always the optimist, always the "glass is half full" guy in the locker room. We pitchers learned from him; Drysdale, Podres, Craig, and Koufax all had the good fortune of pitching to Roy in their early years.

This team had played in a variety of ballparks over the years, but one look at the Memorial Coliseum and pitchers cringed at the dimensions down each foul line. Right field was 300 feet, and it was a minuscule 250 down the left-field line. But there were oceans of green in the right-center and left-center outfields, as the park was vast.

The hitters took one look at the 440 feet sign in deep right center and realized that it was a place mainly designed for football. We all saw one hundred thousand empty seats. What a contrast to Ebbets Field and its cozy thirty-four-thousand-seat stadium with bandbox dimensions in all directions.

Opening Day was another contrast. I pitched to a crowd of almost eighty thousand in 1958. This was not a baseball crowd; it was a curious crowd. The crowd didn't know the team. They had only heard about the stars. It was a historic day as people came to be identified with the first major-league game in Los Angeles. They would keep their ticket stubs to show their grandkids.

The players were equally as curious about the crowd. In about the third inning I looked over from the mound toward our dugout. Several of the Dodgers were gawking over the dugout to see Bing Crosby, Danny Kaye, Lana Turner, Jeff Chandler, and a long list of other Hollywood celebrities. There was no more Dodger Symphony and no catcalls: "Tro it tru his head, I'm witch ya, Cal!"

The crowd was subdued—just watching to see what happened—with no leather-lunged fans like Ebbets Field faithful Hilda Chester. But baseball here was first-class—and a new Dodgers history was beginning.

I'll never forget that first game in L.A., when John Roseboro was catching me, not Campy. The rookie was so pumped up that his first few return throws to me almost hit me in the face. I called time and in front of eighty thousand people motioned for John to step toward the mound. To relieve his tension and put him at ease, I said, "Hey, John, the catcher isn't supposed to throw harder than the pitcher."

The old guard was in its final days. In June of 1959, with the team in fifth place after a seventh-place finish in 1958, management had to make some moves. Pee Wee had already retired and had become a coach. I voluntarily retired, sensing I'd be pushed out any minute, and management reached into its deep minor-league system and brought up Maury Wills, Frank Howard, Larry Sherry, Norm Sherry, and Roger Craig, and they traded for Chuck Essegian. This group, along with a few remnants mentioned in *The Boys of Summer*—Gil Hodges and Duke Snider—won the National League pennant and beat the Chicago White Sox in the 1959 World Series.

When the Dodgers moved to Chavez Ravine, that too was an entirely new experience. Dodger Stadium had lots more foul territory than Ebbets Field. It was more of a pitcher's ballpark. Right field was no Ebbets Field, and left field was certainly not like Wrigley or any of the other bandbox ballparks. It was a culture shock to us former Brooklyn Dodgers. But to the new guys it was a different ballpark, a different era, and this was a good thing.

We were gone; *they* were now.

Duke Snider got the first hit at Chavez Ravine, only fitting for the Duke of Flatbush to come to L.A. and show some grit. Campy was on hand as well that inaugural day, and he remained a spring-training instructor for the Dodgers and went to as many home games as possible.

Roy's first wife couldn't handle his paralysis, and she soon, in the midst of a split, passed away. Roy later on remarried; his new wife, Roxy, adopted his kids, and he adopted hers, and they had one big family. Roxy was Roy's angel. She devoted the rest of her life to being his caregiver and constant companion.

Campy never forgot that I was player rep, as he always called me when he had a deal cooking. "Carl, this guy wants to do this deal . . ." he'd start off, and I'd smile on the other end of the phone.

I was glad that Campy had that type of trust in me. I know that I had that type of trust in him whenever he laid down a sign for me in his crouched position behind the plate. I truly loved that man, but for more personal reasons.

"I worry about you and Betty and Jimmy," he'd tell me whenever we got together. And sometimes he'd call out of the blue to find out how young Jim was faring.

Here was a man who was cut down in the prime of life, and he was asking about my son with Down syndrome. Tears filled my eyes every time I heard his voice asking about Jimmy. But Campy was always positive.

He was a living Job, a prophet of strength right out of the Bible. Job had everything, and when tested with the loss of children and suffering at home, he never cursed God. He questioned why this was happening to him, but he never quit. Campy was my living Job. He questioned, but he never quit. In fact, he'd tell me till his dying day, "Carl, I'm going to whip this chair because it's just between me and God now."

The courage Campy displayed to come back to baseball and coach and to instruct the young players—both catchers and position players—and give tips on hitting was a testament to his character. In the documentary *The Boys of Summer* there is a clip of Rick Monday and Campy laughing together—generations apart in age, hearts together. It was the Campanella way of living. His verve for living and for lecturing on paralysis and telling quadriplegics never to give up made him more than a Hall of Famer. It made him a real man of medicine in my book.

Even the last time I saw Roy, he said to me, "Carl, I always pray for you, Betty, and Jimmy."

Good-bye, Buddy. Your works on this earth will never be forgotten, and your spirit has enveloped the souls of all of us who loved you.

12

Saying Good-Bye to Baseball
as I Knew It

WE HAD SAID OUR GOOD-BYES to old Ebbets Field and landed in Los Angeles, were greeted by Congresswoman Wyman and other dignitaries, and were escorted to our new surroundings. Bringing baseball to the West Coast was a smart business move by Walter O'Malley. Baseball now was a truly national pastime in more than name.

The 1958 season was a year of spring training for all of us in a social sense—except for Duke and Drysdale, who were from California—just to learn the new surroundings. How ironic it was that Duke should be the recipient of a welcome mat, being a native Californian, when we played the Giants.

The funniest moment of all came as we played our first game, the first all–West Coast game in baseball history, at Seals Stadium, a minor-league park (the opening of Candlestick Park was still two years away). Our team was more than pumped to play our old rivals this particular day. We had to win this all-California event, a rematch of New York archenemies.

But the game took a backseat to what happened to Duke when he first stepped off the bus and onto San Francisco soil as a Dodger. Every time we played the Giants at the old Polo Grounds in Brooklyn there would be this disheveled gentleman in an overcoat with a rolled-up newspaper under his arm sitting in dead center field behind Duke Snider, yelling at him. And Duke would complain like a baby to us in the car ride from the Polo Grounds when he, Pee Wee, Rube, and I carpooled home together back in 1956.

"That guy called me 'Horseface' again today! Every game, every season," Duke would say. "And what burns me up is he's sitting there in an overcoat in July with a rolled-up newspaper under his arm and that greasy look about him and he's the one taunting me." Pee Wee glanced back at Duke and said, "I kind of see that!"

"Ah, c'mon!" Duke said, annoyed at the situation, but still trying not to be too serious. It was Pee Wee's way of telling Duke not to let some fan get to him, especially since the Giants were talking of leaving the Polo Grounds and one day he'd be rid of that fan. But, nevertheless, that guy did get to him. And the guy knew right then and there in the stands that he had Duke's ego in the palm of his hand and so he'd sit there in center field and call Duke "Horseface" every game.

The last time we faced the Giants at the Polo Grounds, Duke had one parting thought. "I'll finally be rid of that guy now," he said with his inimitable smile

Our team bus pulled into Seals Stadium, stopped, opened its metal doors, and let us out. Police barricades kept the swelling sold-out crowd in tow, and we exited the bus.

And who should we hear welcome Duke Snider when we stepped off the bus? None other than our old friend.

"Hey, Horseface! You thought you got rid of me, didn't you?" And there he was!

We couldn't believe it. It was the same fan with the same tan overcoat and a rolled-up newspaper under his arm looking just as disheveled as ever. Even Duke had to turn to me and laugh a bit.

One of my last moments of pure fun came on the golf course in 1958, my last full season in the big leagues. If anybody would have told me that 1958 would be my last in the majors, I wouldn't have believed it.

I don't know if fans know how great a golfer Jackie was, but he had a handicap under ten. I used to golf with him on off days. But because he was a four-sport letterman, it didn't surprise me that he was so gifted in golf—it was just another sport for Jackie to learn and quickly master.

The best golfer on the team, however, was Pee Wee Reese. It wasn't even a contest for me when I shot alongside Pee Wee because he was a scratch golfer.

Our schedule might go fifty or sixty games before an off day, but at home or on the road Pee Wee would always arrange a golf game—usually with borrowed clubs and shoes. He would shoot in the low seventies every time.

But Jackie was two years removed from his Dodgers playing days. He was now golfing more than ever in the business world but was no longer in the locker room with us, which saddened us all.

It was now up to Pee Wee, me, and Duke to continue the road golf outings whenever possible. But that became rather tenuous. Unlike Charlie Dressen, who was known to carry a set of clubs with him and who could likewise drive a good ball, Walter Alston had a different view of golf outings, similar to that of Casey Stengel.

Yogi Berra once recounted how Casey Stengel, when he took over the team, said, "After spring training, leave your clubs home."

Walter Alston saw eye to eye with Casey on the subject of golf clubs being better left in their bags at home. Once the season began, the tee shots ended, in Walter's book.

But there was one day during the 1958 season when not even Walter could keep a good game down. We began a series with our archrival Giants in San Francisco, and I knew from the start that this was not going to be just another Friday.

The games were set up so that we had a day game, followed by a night game, and then another day game.

"Come on, Carl, get your clubs!" a frantic Pee Wee whispered to me in the locker room after our day game, gesturing that I should put a move on it and get ready to bolt out of there.

"I can't. You know the rule," I said, matter-of-factly.

"Get dressed already!" Pee Wee pleaded, gesturing like mad as if Big Brother was about to walk in on our discussion.

"We're not supposed to be playing golf," I pleaded with him, desperately wanting to play in my heart.

"We're golfing!" he demanded.

"I really shouldn't be out there," I tried to interrupt. He had none of it.

"That broken arm of yours won't get any worse!" Pee Wee said. I had a sore arm and had by this time already begun thinking of ending my career. Pee Wee convinced me to let loose and play some golf, that it couldn't possibly hurt my arm any more.

He was right. The deal was made. The plan was set in motion.

The next day we golfed at Pebble Beach, one of the toughest courses anyone will ever play—and we weren't even playing the pro tees. We were playing from the regulation tees. I broke a hundred. Duke shot better. Dressen shot pretty well. Pee Wee blasted us all—hitting fairways, staying out of trouble, and holing 'em out when it counted.

The cowhide was a different story.

Retirement is never fun, but it's a necessity. It's an executive decision that must be carried out. Only the team often hopes the player will be his own commander in chief at that point in time.

I often quipped to myself that, unlike other guys, I would know when to hang 'em up. Well, I was wrong. I had arm trouble. I knew I was finished. It was only a matter of how and when. I was always told I would know when to take off my uniform. I always thought they'd have to tear it off me, but I was wrong.

The Dodgers, true to their form, did let me bow out gracefully, which is another concern for all players. No player wants to be traded away or dismissed as if he meant nothing to the organization. The Dodgers gave me a tremendous amount of respect, and I'm grateful to Walter O'Malley and Buzzy for that.

I walked into Buzzy Bavasi's office on June 15, 1959, and told him that I was finished.

Fans often ask me how I *knew*. It's as if my arm told me, "Carl, we can't do it any more." It was as simple as that.

Pee Wee was gone as a player. Jackie was the first to leave us, and then Campy had his tragic car accident. Koufax and Drysdale were young kids and doing well. Koufax was a phenomenon in the making, and Big D was already garnering television coverage. Don Drysdale understood the game and the art of Robinson intimidation.

Don Drysdale once said, "If he's thinking curve, and I'm thinking in, look out!" He knew his craft. The changing of the guard is never a pleasant or easy moment, but I knew that the Dodgers would be in good hands. Big D knew what it took to win, and I knew that Don and Sandy would deliver the Dodgers many World Series championships.

Don Newcombe had been traded to Cincinnati; Furillo had been released. Now just remnants of the Boys of Summer remained: the Duke, Gilliam, and Gil Hodges were the last of us original '55 guys left.

It wasn't just a bad outing that whispered in my ear and told me I was through. It was a series of them—a series of snowflakes that made for a terrible blizzard I couldn't dig myself out of.

"Don't do anything yet," the guys pleaded with me—Koufax, Drysdale, Duke, and Pee Wee (now a coach). "You still have good stuff," they'd tell me after I threw batting practice. "Don't quit."

I listened.

The "Steel City" was icy cold to me. I struck out the Pirates' Bill Virdon and all seemed well. Maybe I shouldn't retire, I thought. Maybe I was going to be OK. Maybe the guys were right.

These thoughts raced through my head, and then crashed and burned.

A few bloop hits ensued, and then Dick Stuart took me deep.

"It's just not your day," a consoling Walter Alston told me when his spikes reached the mound and I looked up at his face.

"Walt, this is the last time you'll have to come to the mound for me," I told him, fighting back the emotions.

I was done, officially done.

Roger Craig, who had helped us win the 1955 World Series as a bright-eyed kid, was now twenty-nine and took my spot in the rotation. He proceeded to win eleven games for the Dodgers the rest of that season and helped them get back to the World Series.

But Buzzy had plans for me and for my graceful departure.

"I don't want to let the club release you," Buzzy Bavasi told me in his office.

"You won't have to," I assured Buzzy. "I'm retiring!"

I was paid the rest of the 1959 season and became a coach for the Dodgers, which afforded me a bird's-eye seat for the '59 World Series. I tore a page out of Jackie's book and really enjoyed watching the new kids win it all against the White Sox.

End of an old era, dawn of a new one: so go the seasons—fall is when old trees lean on younger branches, making way for a spring when new seeds sprout.

Jackie and I corresponded well after our playing days were over, as he was a founding member of Freedom National Bank in Harlem and I had found a new career at First National Bank back home in Anderson.

Jackie wrote me at the decade's end about "the ongoing struggle." I knew what he meant. He was only three full seasons removed from the game, but he never referenced his baseball career. We shared the philosophy that life must move onward.

In 1960—my first year out of pro ball—I received a request to meet with Dale W. McMillen—founder and chairman of Central Soya Company of Fort Wayne, Indiana. Mr. Mac had developed his livestock feed company into an internationally successful business.

He was quite wealthy, and he enjoyed sharing his wealth with those less fortunate. He contributed to numerous worthy causes, donating to schools, churches, and parks in the Fort Wayne area. He observed one day, while watching Little League tryouts at McMillen Park, the harsh fact that only 20 percent of the kids would make it. The other 80 percent went home. It troubled him, and he wanted to get the kids to feel that they all were a part of the game, and so he approached me to help him start his Wildcat League. The name came from the mascot for Central Soya.

We brought that venture to fruition, and I held instructional baseball clinics in parks all over Fort Wayne. Five thousand kids responded. At the end of the season Mr. Mac wanted to bring all of these kids together in one place for "Progress Day."

"Carl," he said. "Get me Jackie Robinson. I want him to come here and be a part of it all. We have lots of black kids in this program."

I asked Jackie if he'd come, and the next thing I knew he was at my doorstep in Anderson, and he kept returning to Progress Day year after year, bringing other top names with him. Mr. Mac named Jackie and me the "Godfathers" of Wildcat Baseball.

There was one unfinished piece of business to attend to in 1961: the official good-bye to Ebbets Field. I flew in from Anderson to attend that funeral.

Dressed in slacks and a collared shirt, I stood inside cold Ebbets Field on that fateful day. Its face and time are of no consequence now. Its memory rears its head every time the phrase Subway Series is mentioned, every time I get a phone call from a frantic *New York Post, New York Times,* or *New York Daily News* reporter trying to tweak my brain for a Dodgers-Yankees reflection. But as

I said before, I will *never* concede that we were dominated by those Yankees.

I noticed, as I stood on the beautiful green field one last time, a large, white wrecking ball, with red stitches perfectly etched around it, ominously resting high above my head.

A short ceremony was followed by shorter glances all around Ebbets Field and then one last look at my teammates who could emotionally stand to attend the service—Campy in his wheelchair, myself, Branca, and Tommy Holmes. Jackie did not attend the farewell.

The brevity of the ceremony was fitting and yet painful. It was fitting because everyone was choked up, and painful because that little park gave its heart and soul to our club and represented a great portion of our lives, our rites of passage, and now it was about to be gone without any fanfare—a less-than-comforting twist on life.

The engine on the crane roared louder than the crowd had the entire last year. My eyes affixed themselves across the diamond on the visitors' dugout. I remembered the players, the fans, the cheers, the games won—and suddenly the baseball resting above my head started to sway back and forth. A man inside the crane manipulated that large white wrecking ball.

I ran my eight-millimeter home movie camera, looking through the eyepiece as the ball struck the visitors' dugout—the roof of the dugout falling sickly into the dugout pit—and I walked out of the park for the last time.

The days of Duke and I parking our cars in the lot on Bedford Avenue and worrying about baseballs hit out onto it were gone.

The days of going to the diner on Empire Boulevard and talking with the fans over some coffee were gone. The place that made life seem so good was about to be demolished.

When I boarded my plane back to Indiana, I felt incredibly sick. It was as if I had lost a member of the family. I couldn't believe that the beautiful grass that we once trotted over during warm-ups was now just tall weeds barely resembling any shade of green.

All I could think about was how unprepared, emotionally, I was for this situation. Ebbets Field looked the sick patient. It was pale, losing color every second, and had given up its will to survive.

I was soon engrossed once again in helping out youth clinics, when I wasn't involved in banking, and found that extremely rewarding emotionally—knowing that I made a difference to youngsters' lives. Looking back on it, the difference I made in kids' lives was not unlike that of many of my fellow teammates, but the difference Jackie made was of epic proportions. Dreams lived and died with Robinson, Doby, Campy, Newk, and the great African-American men who followed, such as Willie Mays and Hank Aaron.

One year when Jackie visited the Wildcat Baseball clinic, he brought Rachel with him. The event ended up being a great reunion for our wives. It was also a great event for the Wildcat children from all over Fort Wayne. Incidentally, my family doctor today is Philip Goshert, M.D., a Wildcat kid in 1961 at McMillen Park whom I taught to bunt.

The program of Wildcat Baseball is still running strong today, thanks to a foundation set up by Mr. Mac, who has since passed on, and thanks to Jackie's initial support of the program and giving of his time. Always available for those of us he considered close to him, Jackie graciously gave of his time and did it with a smile.

The business side of Jackie Robinson flourished after his early retirement from the game. He brought the same type of tenacity to the banking business that he brought to the base paths. It was clearly evident to me upon first look at Jackie in action that business life was an easy second love of his.

Chock Full o' Nuts coffee company approached Jackie to become an officer in the company, and he became personnel director. Not wanting to turn down a platform through which to get the message of civil rights and equality across to the changing New York City demographic, Jackie seized the opportunity. He took a hard stand that he couldn't take in baseball and used that to excel in an executive position in corporate America.

Stepping away from the game, it seemed rather ironic that he was bringing the entire business world closer to it. His acumen rubbed off on everyone around him. Freedom National Bank, a charter National Bank in the 1960s, asked Jackie to assist them in developing housing projects and small businesses in Harlem. Jackie saw this as a chance to gain a platform. He was correct. In the process he drew inner-city youngsters into both the political and sports arenas. This was also a time when other sports, such as golf and tennis, were commanding attention, but Jackie remained loyal to baseball and kept up his appearances to further the marketing of baseball as more of a racially blind sport. Because most country clubs were restricted at that time, golf was not about to take over as a national pastime. President Eisenhower made golf the elite sport that it is today, and Arnold Palmer and Jack Nicklaus took the ball from the president and ran with the endorsement opportunities.

I was a businessman now in Anderson and tried to forget about baseball to some degree. I wasn't trying to abandon the game, but I was trying to prove to myself that I could succeed in the business world on my own.

During the mid-1960s I had invited Jackie to speak at another community function in Anderson, and he obliged. I met him at the Indianapolis Airport, where he had flown in from Louisville. He looked unnerved—perturbed about something—but I didn't press the issue. I simply asked him how the trip was from Louisville and how everything went with his speech.

The day before, he had spoken at a function on Pee Wee's behalf, and when we got into my car and had said our hellos to one another, Jackie began to unload.

"Carl, you won't believe what happened in Louisville!" Jackie said. "After my speech, in which I had many good things to say about Pee Wee and his support as a teammate and how much I admired him, there was a press conference," Jack continued.

I didn't interrupt. I listened, waiting with an impending sense of disaster.

"Things went fine until I got this question: 'What do you think about your teammate Pee Wee owning a bowling alley here in Louisville that's segregated?'" Jackie relayed to me, still stunned.

"I was caught completely off guard," he told with me without a pause.

"But, Carl, it's true. How could it be?" Jackie asked me.

I saw my friendships with those two men flash before my eyes. I saw the "baseball" Pee Wee accept Jackie in record time. I also saw the social side of things in which Jackie was slowly being accepted.

I assured Jackie that Pee Wee was involved in the bowling alley in name only—and that the sign outside the alley was where the relationship between him and the other investors in the alley who supported that policy ended.

"It's only a matter of time until segregation will disappear, Jack," I said, but I knew in my heart he was unmoved.

Although not at all satisfied with my answer, he nevertheless accepted my comments out of true friendship.

The incident in Louisville did not affect Jackie's friendship with Pee Wee in the slightest. Jackie made no issue out of it with Pee Wee because he knew that Pee Wee's respect for him was genuine. Pee Wee wasn't two-faced. The bowling alley reflected the disparity in the speed at which baseball accepted Jackie Robinson as opposed to society at that time in 1960. Society was years behind, and Pee Wee was being used as an athlete for his name on that bowling alley. Pee Wee too was a sharp businessman and had several investments in Louisville.

This was still an era in which the writers controlled the game's mass media, which back in 1960 still meant newspapers and syndication. There wasn't any ESPN or televised games on any sort of regular basis. The writers had accepted Jackie back in 1947 by voting him National League Rookie of the Year. But thirteen years after his debut, baseball was still far ahead of society, which had done little to nothing from a governmental standpoint to advance civil rights. This incident in Louisville was another reminder to Jackie, as if he needed any more, of the long path toward true equality in this country.

During that ride from the airport to Anderson, Jackie told me that the speech he had prepared was in transcript form—and that all of his speeches were read. He said he couldn't take a chance at being quoted or misquoted with off-the-cuff remarks. I looked at him rather wistfully because I wished that weren't the case.

The next time I had a chance to visit with Jackie alone and out of earshot of any press or former teammates, he shared something even more unbelievable with me.

The Vietnam War was raging in full force in 1969. Unlike World War II, it divided this country. It wasn't spring, when new flowers grew. It was stark winter. There wasn't a united America the way there had been with the Greatest Generation, as Tom Brokaw showed us.

Vietnam was an unpopular war, to say the least.

Countless parents who had fought in World War II were against this war. No matter what a person's political views were at the time, everybody was hoping and praying our soldiers would come back uninjured.

Jackie's prayers were answered in that his son did return, but he came home a far cry from the young lad whom Jackie had hugged good-bye. Jackie Jr. was a gentle, sweet kid with a heart of gold and a love of life. He returned bitter and with a drug problem. This broke Jackie's heart. He made Jackie Jr. seek counseling and rehabilitation. Just as the "promised land" was reached, as Jackie Jr. was successfully treated and was embarking on a normal life, a tragic day occurred in the Robinson household. Jackie learned that his son was killed in a car accident. "Carl, when I think of all of the hours I spent with other people's children in classrooms and in youth clinics, I should have been spending more time with my own kids," he wistfully said to me.

I tried my best to console him.

"Jackie, you gave your kids a great life," I told him.

But I knew that it didn't console him. I knew he was forever a broken and devastated man. Whenever we addressed youth clinics, he was a dead man walking once he looked at all of those young faces. All parents live with the fear of the death of a child, and so each time Jackie did one of these appearances it hurt all the more because one of his children had died so young.

"Most of us have felt that way in our heart of hearts—that we should have spent more time with our kids," Clem Labine reflected.

But if Jackie had it to do over again, he probably would have spent the same number of hours helping others' kids and helping to save lives—which he did. These kids listened to him as if he spoke gospel. He spoke and they obeyed. Lives that would have been lost to the streets were saved and made productive. Jackie's influence has been spread like seeds, with young stalks growing everywhere.

13
Autumn Men

IT WAS THE SPRING OF 1972 — seventeen years after we had finally won Brooklyn its only World Series.

For all of us — Duke, Jackie, Pee Wee, Campy, and myself — it seemed as if it all happened yesterday. The "Boys of Summer" were gray-haired "Men of Autumn."

Ebbets Field was a distant memory. An apartment complex stood in its place. Roger Kahn made us feel youthful again by writing his touching tribute to us, *The Boys of Summer*. Only now we were together not in the dugout or clubhouse at Ebbets Field. Tavern on the Green was the congregating forum this particular day — the debut party of Roger's book. The entire team showed up, ready to play. All of the personalities in the book were there. I stood off to one side talking to Jackie. He was a little heavy, and his hair had turned completely gray.

I asked Jackie about his golf game, and while I asked him I immediately thought about how he could beat most of the guys not only in golf, but in Ping-Pong, tennis, poker, and bridge — not to mention hearts, which he played on the train with Ernie Harwell. Ernie used to marvel at how competitive Jackie was off the field, even in a friendly game of hearts. But that was the fire inside of him. It's what stoked his abilities to flourish in all of their glory.

We were interrupted by a patient young lady who shyly walked over to ask Jackie for his autograph. He obliged with a smile but turned to me and said, "Carl, start my hand on the page. I'm afraid I'll run off the edge." He wasn't kidding. This was the first time I realized that diabetes had taken the sight from this gifted man. There are some things in life that cause even the mightiest of men to fall, and diabetes makes no exceptions.

Rachel told me that Jackie was not taking care of the diabetes properly; he was running around way too much, helping out in inner cities with lots of travel for civil rights events. While diabetes was wracking his body, he still held his vice president position at Chock Full o' Nuts as personnel director. He was still courting Richard Nixon, the Kennedy family, Nelson Rockefeller, and everybody who would stand up and fight for civil rights. He still had that sense of urgency. Even though the light was going dim in his own life, he wanted a better life for others. In fact, I think the fact that he was so ill made him even more impatient with the process.

He knew that few men had the energy he had. He knew few men had the stature to be able to bring about any change. His contacts in the political, athletic, and social arenas were unparalleled.

Rachel pleaded with him, to no avail, to curtail his hectic schedule, right up until the World Series in 1972.

The doctors pleaded with him, too, but when Jackie had set his mind to something, there was no turning back. Bigots were causing major impediments to the civil rights movement with church bombings and violence in the streets, and Jackie knew that, in the twilight of his life, he needed to make sure the stones were set in place to pave the way for a better tomorrow. But for us, as our teammate and friend, Jackie was fading fast—too fast for those of us who loved him.

That was the last time I'd ever see him.

Before he passed, Jackie did finish one piece of business, though—his running feud in the newspapers with Jim Murray of the *L.A. Times.*

Jackie attended the 1972 World Series in Cincinnati and met Jim face-to-face. It had been some years since their newspaper duels, and Jackie extended his hand to Jim and said, "Sorry, Jim. I can't see you anymore."

This was the last time the world saw Jackie Robinson.

Right after he attended that 1972 World Series in Cincinnati, Jackie was gone—October 24, 1972. It was a shock to all of us. We always thought of Jackie as this strong, superhuman athlete, and he died blind and in a lot of pain. This seemed like the cruelest blow of all to this man who had sacrificed himself at every stage for the benefit of society. These last years of Jackie's life—his early fifties—should have been the prime of his life, his glory years, to enjoy retirement and golf and have fun with his family and friends.

Jim Murray, upon hearing the news of Jackie's death, was so devastated that Jackie had suffered to the end from blindness caused by advanced diabetes that he wrote a column about their final meeting and what Jackie meant to the game. He closed his column with a rather poignant, "I'm sorry, Jackie, I can't see you anymore."

Jackie Robinson's funeral was held in New York City—a Baptist funeral—and Reverend Jesse Jackson presided. It was a somber moment for all of us who attended, and it was packed with loved ones. All I could think about was that our superstar, the man who epitomized the Brooklyn Dodgers, was gone. Rev. Jackson gave a strong sermon. He closed his eulogy by saying about Jackie, "He got tired. He stole home."

The reverend used the occasion to carry the torch for civil rights, which Jackie would have wanted, but I thought that one point that someone should have emphasized was the fact that Jackie gave momentum to the civil rights movement in modern times by reenergizing it and setting it upon a new, strong course. I believe Jackie single-handedly kicked off the civil rights movement, but it would have been nice if someone phrased it that way.

The start of the movement, to me, is the most important aspect of any work in progress. Civil rights is still a work in progress, but Jackie started it way back on April 15, 1947, by stepping between the tightly etched white lines of a baseball batter's box and waiting for that first pitch. I couldn't believe that the strong-willed man that I had known so well and for so long was now being laid to rest. Life is unfair at times. One minute Jackie was stealing home. The next minute home plate was being taken away from him.

Jackie enjoyed witnessing the advancement of civil rights, and he didn't care which political party took the credit as long as it did something to further the cause. Jackie was aligned with anybody and everybody who took a strong position for civil rights. He went back and forth between parties until he saw one party move forward. Eisenhower espoused good things, but he never was effective in getting civil rights legislation passed. So Jackie sided with Nelson Rockefeller. Jackie didn't care for JFK's oscillation at first, but Robert Kennedy jumped on the cause, and Jackie backed him wholeheartedly. Jackie was apolitical but had a zeal for life, liberty, and equal rights.

At this point in the early 1970s, Betty and I were facing our own battle with America as we knew it over our own son, Jimmy. Jimmy was born with Down syndrome, and America at that time was not kind to anyone with a disability. All we met at every step of the way were defensive attitudes. But there was an unspoken but understood support for Betty and me from my teammates. Catcher Del Crandall of the Milwaukee Braves, who had two handicapped sons of his own, shared some thoughts with me and also offered support.

I had two families—my blood family and my Dodgers family. One I lived with; the other was gone but not forgotten—and I wanted to go back to Brooklyn to have one more stroll around the old neighborhood.

In 2000 I made that journey from Indiana to Brooklyn once more. I needed to do this—as the guys were almost all gone now. I just had to go back, if only for one last look around.

I thought of those of us who were left—me, Labine, Snider, Podres, Branca, and Koufax.

Duke Snider was now retired from broadcasting. He had been an announcer with the Montreal Expos for quite a number of years and was now content to enjoy sunny California. But whether he's in Brooklyn or Los Angeles, he'll always be the Duke of Flatbush to our loyal fans, and that's what has been lost—the togetherness of Brooklyn. The team mattered to the locals in Brooklyn. We were a part of their extended family. Playing my career in Brooklyn reaffirmed the idea that a baseball team can be a form of identification for a fan, a sense of belonging, and a sense of vicarious camaraderie. But now the team had lost much of its nucleus. The fans themselves were fading into voices of the past. The ushers I knew were gone. The ticket takers, many of whom had passed on, were a vision of the past. And so we all became men and women of autumn. It was only fitting. We had grown up together, raised our families together, shopped together at the local food stores, bought meat together from Joe Rossi, and gone to Cosmo's for haircuts together. In the following of Dylan Thomas, many of the friends from Brooklyn did not "go gentle into that good night." Jackie fought hard till the end, both his disease and for social equality. Campanella lived every day to its fullest, even though he needed a housemaid to help him in and out of his wheelchair. Furillo was a tough Italian kid from Pennsylvania farm country, and he fought cancer like he guarded Abe Stark's sign. It was unfortunate that for all of the guarding of that sign, he was never given a suit.

Pee Wee Reese, our captain, had passed away in 1999, leaving a vacancy never to be filled. It seemed as if the rest of the infield was gone as well, prompting Duke to quip to Pee Wee in the late 1990s, "I hope none of that spreads to the outfield."

Big D had left us way too soon. Don Drysdale died of a heart attack in his fifties, another fiery Robinson-type leaving us only his uniform number in 1993. Ironically, this was the same year Roy Campanella passed away, and these were losses that devastated the Dodgers organization and all of baseball because both men were links to the past and bridged many generations of diehards.

What was left at the turn of the twenty-first century was a small and lonely group of us. And so when I was asked to make an appearance at the New York Downtown Athletic Club to honor longtime athletic director Rudy Riska in 2000, I just knew this would be a perfect occasion to gather the entire family and truck them to New York with me.

I wanted just one more season in the sun. I attended the ceremony, and the day after the event I rented a van and driver and took them all back to Brooklyn. The driver was a young man who didn't know the area, and so I became our tour guide by dint of elimination. The road system made the neighborhood look different. It was as if we were headed to a foreign place I'd never seen. I directed him first to Empire Boulevard and then to Bedford Avenue, the site of old Ebbets Field. Only this area looked familiar. And once more the emotions started flowing as I looked at an apartment complex wall where a ball should have been bouncing off. Sometimes it's best to go back, and sometimes it's best not to, and this was one time in my life that I was torn between both emotions as I stood there gazing at our old wall, now just a structural buttress.

As we all stood in a Kentucky Fried Chicken parking lot across Bedford Avenue—behind where the right-field fence used to stand and where players parked their cars in a filling station—I couldn't believe that Ebbets Field could have fit into that small piece of real estate. When I first saw the park as a rookie, I admired its breadth. When I saw Ralph Kiner or Stan Musial home runs fly out of there like sick birds, I wanted to push that short right-field fence back to the gas station beyond yonder way.

A thirty-story apartment complex and a Little League diamond called "Ebbets Field" occupied the historic space in 2000. It just didn't look right. Then we drove to Coney Island. Thank God that Nathan's was still there. I don't know if I could have controlled myself if they had torn down Nathan's.

I walked up to the old-style windows, still metal-edged and flush against the wall as I once knew. I leaned over and asked for my Nathan's hot dog, as in olden times. The hot dog even tasted the same as it had in 1951. I knew this wasn't just a snack. It was a moment to be savored, and so I took that hot dog, munching every step of the way, and walked along the boardwalk with a cool and easy stride. I looked up at the Cyclone, took in the parachute jump, and reflected on a life in baseball while taking in the views of the beach. The Atlantic Ocean looked the same. The kids were playing—a new generation with only a parent's or grandparent's connection to us old guys.

But the memories all came back. I saw the kids walking in the sand, and in each child I saw one of our children, whether it was Duke's daughter, my son, Preacher's kids, Millie and Rube Walker's children, or Clem's son, Jay. The names were different, but the verve for life was the same. I thought that if those kids would have been at the helm in baseball, Jackie would have played a lot sooner.

Brooklyn was a true borough with both citified life and beach life. Our kids could go to the local store in just a few minutes by foot or have us drive ten minutes and be playing in the sand at the beach or riding the Cyclone on a Friday night. The memories felt fresh, as if they had happened yesterday.

The biggest step of the entire journey was my decision to drive by the old neighborhood. But I insisted, and we moved on and headed for my old neighborhood in Bay Ridge. The streets hadn't changed a bit. The houses were beautiful. The rows looked as straight as ever, the sidewalks as clean as ever. The fun memories came back once more. Duke was outside on the lawn. Preacher was barbecuing, and Rube was talking to the kids. Pee Wee was signing an autograph, and I was taking in the sun. Only different men lived here now. My buddies were forty-five years removed from Bay Ridge and Brooklyn paradise.

Oh, the memories. There was Cosmo's Barber Shop and Joe Rossi's Butcher Shop. Joe had continued to supply me with veal cutlets long after I had moved to Indiana. Then there was good old Abe Myerson, the deli owner—who made a phenomenal hero. These folks were all family to us. But the more I walked and saw the changed guard, the more they now seemed light years away.

Junior's Cheesecake, though, was still in business. Casa Bianca was a great Italian restaurant in Bay Ridge. Lundy's out in Long Island was noisy and great for the families, and they had excellent food. The buckets of clams they brought to this flatlander from Indiana gave me an education in dining.

Duke, PeeWee, Rube Walker, and Preacher Roe had all lived near our place on Lafayette Walk, which is on Ninety-fourth Street between Third and Fourth Avenues in Bay Ridge. It was central to everything—friends and stores alike—a neighborhood with character. Brooklyn had the butcher who lived down the street, the pharmacist who stayed open later if we needed him to, the baker who was a Dodgers fan and remembered our birthdays. It was like living in a small town. Kids today can't fathom that because city life and country life are so vastly different.

After Levittown was built in the late 1950s, a family had two choices: the city life or the pure rural life. There was only suburbia or the city. There wasn't any middle ground. Brooklyn had been that ephemeral middle ground. It was rural in aspects—beach-filled with crisp, clean, ocean breezes—and also had a strong cultural base.

But after 1956, a family either moved to the country and needed an automobile for everything, or they stayed in the city and lived among the hustle and bustle. Neighborhoods such as Bay Ridge, Flatbush, Williamsburg, Rego Park, and Forest Hills were a dying breed. After the turn of the new century these neighborhoods came back a bit, but that was well after Ebbets Field was a thought of the past.

My son Gary was age six when we left Brooklyn in 1957. It was amazing to me how much a six-year-old took in at that time of life, but those Brooklyn years made quite an impression on young Gary.

He stood for a long time looking behind the row houses where the garages were at a lower level—a cement area with garages and houses. He loved his old ball diamond, where he and his older brother Danny played with their pink, soft-rubber Spalding and broomstick. He remembered it well.

Stickball was a city tradition for years—and I hope it never dies out. It's the only game where home runs are counted based on sewers! No country kid could ever get that at home. It's the only game where the mothers of the kids would yell out of the windows of the houses for the kids to come in—and you can't get that on a diamond in the country in the middle of nowhere either.

That day in 2000, however, Gary was a bit misty-eyed. He understood what he had lived through and how special that Robinson team was in Brooklyn, and he turned to me and said, "Hey, Dad, look. There was a single, back there a double—on the roof a home run!"

Then, looking at the many clotheslines stretched across the open area, he said, "And if you hit a pair of pants it was two runs!"

For a minute we had that look in our eyes of "just one more game," but that was not to happen. Some dreams are dreamt once, and life won't allow them to be relived. This was one such time. Robinson was now long since removed from our abilities to reach out and hug him, and Campy had left us as well. The remaining few of us were all just a bit older in years. And there was our old house—still intact, still looking the same as the day we moved out in 1957.

I still heard the voices of the past—the roaring fans, my long-time buddy, Kenny Smith, usher in Section 9. It was at this point that I wished I could walk inside Ebbets Field, walk into the locker room, undress at my locker, and hear Duke's bawdy sense of humor rearing its head once again. I heard Campy laughing, and I saw Pee Wee looking rather regal in his "captain's chair" in our locker room.

I missed the smell of hot popcorn, and I missed the hot dog vendors with their booming voices. I missed the "Look at me when I talk to you, Branca!" from Hilda Chester.

There were the days when Duke and Newk would playfully get on each other. Duke would go and cut up one of Newk's ties in his locker, and Newk would come back with some tricks of his own. The noise in the clubhouse from those two mouths still shrills inside my head, but that's about all I've got left.

At this point, with a lump in my throat, I was so glad that I had all of the old movies I'd taken on eight-millimeter film.

I have my brother to thank for that, as he urged me to become interested in eight-millimeter movies. He was a photographer, and his enthusiasm for the captured moment rubbed off on me. And so I too played amateur photographer every year in spring training, taking shots of the players and fans during workouts and off days.

I wanted to preserve the precious memory of being a pro ballplayer. Plus our families were growing up together and we took lots of shots of the kids. I had this innate sense that youth was fleeting, and I wanted to have a little keepsake to reflect on during my later years.

I contributed some of my footage to HBO's Black Canyon Productions in New York, who produced "When It Was a Game" using some of my footage and a few other players' home movies.

I thought they did a great job of showing scenes young fans could never have known—such as what Ebbets Field looked like in vibrant color, the suits that the players wore, the lushness of Ebbets Field and the Polo Grounds, and the facade at Yankee Stadium.

One of the memories of Ebbets Field was of Happy Felton and his Knothole Gang. There were three shows each day. First was an early pregame show shot from inside the Dodgers' bullpen. Three Little Leaguers would, at that point, perform a series of throwing and fielding drills, observed by one of the Dodgers. The Dodgers would pick a winner, and that kid got to come back the next day. Then there was the second show shot by the home dugout, and a player was picked for an on-camera interview. The third show, called "Talk to the Stars," was one in which Happy and his assistant Larry McDonald would pick a player from each team as stars of the game. This was a postgame show, and it was a call-in show where fans could call and talk to us. If we were named to any of the three shows, it nabbed us a cool fifty bucks! Pee Wee made so many, all of his teammates claim he was still cashing the checks at age eighty!

It was as if I still saw Happy and his microphone out there somewhere behind the apartment complex where the lush grass used to be—or somewhere between KFC and Bedford Avenue.

I suddenly remembered the time when I was sent in to pinch run for Jackie Robinson—if you can believe that.

I was occasionally called on to pinch run, but never for Jackie.

We were playing the Cubs at Wrigley, and Jackie hit a double and banged his knee in a hard slide at second. He was lifted from the game, and I was called in—a pitcher called in to pinch run. It was the only time in his ten-year career that someone pinch ran for Jackie. I knew at the time it was a rare moment and one I'd want to tell my grandkids about one day. Every time I tell the story I smile and remember all of those good times in Brooklyn, just as

I did with Gary back in the middle of the street looking at the stickball visions of the past. Although nothing extraordinary happened to me on the bases, it was still an honor.

But that was then, this was now. We weren't Boys of Summer. We were Autumn Men. We weren't in the March days of our careers. We were in the Octobers. And it was time to leave and bid my Bay Ridge adieu.

14

Jackie and Jimmy: The Parallel

D O LIFE'S EXPERIENCES actually prepare one for challenges that lie ahead? I certainly believe they do. Johnny Wilson prepared me for Jackie. And Jackie prepared me for my son Jimmy.

America had some of the same social attitudes toward people with disabilities as it had toward race relations. Jackie made people look beyond race, inside their own souls, inside the depths of what made them human, and see the light. In doing so, Jackie likewise changed the way people viewed each other. Jimmy's barriers were physical and mental, and he benefited from Jackie's perseverance and from the momentum generated by Jackie. It was slow at first, but then it gained enough speed to sustain itself.

Jimmy was born after Jackie's career was long since over — at a time when Jackie and I were not teammates anymore and no longer seeing each other daily. But even though the two of them didn't have a routine relationship, Jimmy benefited greatly from my experiences with Jackie. I often felt Jackie came into my life to teach me how to channel energy and anger toward what was happening around me with Jimmy and society's nonacceptance of Down syndrome and other birth defects.

I had played with Jackie for nine seasons, living side by side with him in the clubhouse and on the road. Today I have a forty-four year relationship with my son Jimmy.

After I retired from the game, we were about to permanently move to New York City to take a job with Phillips Van Heusen Company. The plans had been all set, and everything was in motion. My wife, Betty, was pregnant with our fourth child, and when he was born I rushed home to Indiana. I never did take the Van Heusen job.

The word spread rapidly at St. John's Hospital in Anderson: "The Erskine baby is Mongoloid"—a harsh and fearful term in the '50s. Soon after Jimmy's birth, the doctors informed us that he had Down syndrome. The doctors suggested that there were many places where Jimmy could enjoy a nice home and that he would be cared for—but Betty was having none of that. "Jimmy comes home with us! Whatever is needed, he's a part of our family," she said forcefully. She had carried this little guy for nine months and wasn't about to abandon him.

That gave me the courage to go home and sit down with our other three kids—Danny, ten; Gary, eight; and Susan, three—and explain to them that they had a special little brother who was going to need their love and help.

In all the years since, they have done just that. Unashamed, they brought their friends home and treated Jimmy like any kid brother. That was the greatest speech I ever made.

Jackie helped me to encourage other parents whose children had birth defects or physical disabilities or diseases. Jackie had his Rookie of the Year and his Hall of Fame plaque, and my Jimmy went on to earn gold medal after gold medal in the Special Olympics. I wish Jackie had lived to see those days because Jackie had a lot to do with Jim's success.

There is a strong parallel between their experiences. Although each came along at different times and in different social moods, there are huge similarities.

For instance, there is an exclusion aspect similar to both experiences. There is nothing in life so difficult to accept as being left out, whether it's left out of the local ball game or left out of the major leagues or left out of life. They were both excluded, left out of the mainstream, and denied equal access to public places and opportunities.

Jackie and Jimmy, because of tradition, superstition, ignorance, fear, and arrogance, felt the bitterness of rejection. Society considered them second-class citizens, or worse. Fear, misunderstanding, and prejudice ruled the day. Jackie was denied housing in Connecticut when he and Rachel first tried to move there. He was also denied access to hotels and restaurants. Jimmy, and others like him, were denied group homes in real neighborhoods.

One of the hardest experiences of my life was attending meetings in neighborhoods where a group home was being proposed—a home that usually would have eight handicapped men or women plus staff—and have the neighbors resist because, "We don't want these lunatics, sex maniacs, and insane people living next to us. Our property values will drop." That, to me, was a low, low blow. I told one local lady, "We're talking about a group home here, not a landfill!"

The whole Robinson experience, which I had lived through as a player, now seemed to arise in our lives. Jimmy was facing many of the same barriers. Only now I was coping with this experience as a father. Some of those who uttered these terrible words were people I personally knew quite well. I felt a good dose of the pain and rejection Jackie told me he used to feel. The word *tough* doesn't come close to describing how hurtful it was to me. After all, this was my home town; I'd never known how fearful people could be about someone who was different. I used to ask myself, "Why are all these harsh things being said about my son?"

Jimmy didn't do anything to deserve this. But what made the words from fellow townspeople even harsher to me was the fact that I knew some of these people to be good people. I knew that they just didn't understand.

Special education hadn't begun yet in the public schools—not until Jimmy was twelve. Progress was made—but very slowly. Betty and I now fully understood why Jackie hated the expression, "Wait till next year." Rachel had a special sensitivity for Betty, mother to mother. Although the two seldom got together because they lived hundreds of miles apart, when I'd run into Rachel with Jackie at a baseball function, she always expressed great interest in and concern for Jimmy. Betty and I deeply appreciated that concern.

As with Jackie, whenever people met and became well acquainted with Jimmy, their ignorance and personal bigotries went away. But acceptance was slow—too slow for any parent— just as Jackie had told me some decades before Jimmy was born. In America and around the world, the sports arena was a great common denominator. In Jackie's case, it was a perfect spotlight to showcase his abilities and attributes. In Jimmy's case, he could not showcase his athletic ability until Eunice Kennedy Shriver introduced the concept of the Special Olympics to the world in 1968. When the Special Olympics came into being, people around the world began to see Jimmy and the others as participants; up until then, they had always been spectators. People finally had a better understanding of what being fully accepted meant to these special kids and their families.

It is a giant step for mankind to watch the Special Olympics and observe the determination and the effort of these athletes with physical challenges. The real payoff comes when the race is over except for the lone runner or swimmer struggling just to finish, and he or she gets a rousing cheer from the many supportive fans on hand.

"We've come a long way, baby!" Jackie would have said to me if he ever got to see Jimmy compete.

In our own community, things were slowly changing. We witnessed an example of the changes on the first day of school for Jimmy, age twelve, after he boarded the big yellow school bus down at the corner. As the bus pulled away, Betty and I hugged each other and turned to walk back to our house. Our neighbors on both sides of the street, who had been watching from their homes, gave us high fives, thumbs-ups, and loving waves.

Jackie had to be patient in his quest, as Mr. Rickey told him. Rickey's idea that it took more courage for a man not to fight than to fight was rather prophetic. Jackie understood the need to push, but to do so consistently and patiently. This is true for parents of handicapped children as well, as we all had to push and be patient while we were pushing. Parental groups started training centers and workshops. I thought about Jackie and how much rejection he got as a kid growing up in Cairo, Georgia, in the 1930s. Jimmy was in a sheltered workshop in training, but training for what? Nothing was open to him because society hadn't allowed openings to occur. He got low scores on tests. His speech was poor. But one area he scored well in was "on task." Jimmy liked to work, and when he was given an assignment like counting screws or matching colors, he stayed right on top of the job, menial as it was. We always knew Jimmy was smart, but his disability had him trapped.

What convinced Betty and me that Jimmy was not only smart but that he understood a lot more than his expressions or body language indicated was an incident that happened one day at home.

Jimmy's emotions and feelings were normal; he was just physically and mentally different. I knew even the sense of humor was there—just waiting to be brought out. And one day, out it came in the most unusual of ways. Jackie would have been proud.

I had always wanted to teach Jimmy to say "No, thank you" rather than just make an unpleasant sound of disapproval. I kept trying to do it but just wasn't getting through.

Jimmy used to like to run off, at age eight, to Mrs. Lamey's house next door. He liked to shake her back door hard to make her five poodles bark. He loved that high-pitched noise. The problem was that it also set off her security alarm, and the police would come out only to find it was Jimmy. This, of course, embarrassed Betty beyond words. After several occasions, Betty said, "Carl, you have to make Jimmy understand. You have to spank him good when he does that again." I told Jimmy, but I wasn't sure he really understood.

I came home one day, and Betty looked completely stressed out.

He had done it again. He had run to the neighbor's house and set off the alarm. I had warned him. I told him he was in for a good spanking.

"OK, Jim, go upstairs in your bedroom!" I told him. He looked at me, sober as a judge, and said as plain as one can say it, "No, thank you."

I knew that the little guy understood everything. It was just trapped inside of him. I couldn't bring myself to spank him. I was happy that I knew he understood what was going on around him. He just did things his own way, at his own pace.

The workshop finally discovered this same aspect of Jimmy as well. They called us in for an evaluation meeting. Then the staff said they would like to try Jimmy on a real job out in the community. Betty and I listened to this idea in total disbelief. "Our Jimmy on a real-life job?" we thought. But it was so.

We had our reservations at first and asked the counselors, "OK, but do you think he can do it?"

"We know he can do it!" they told us.

Jimmy has been working at Applebee's Restaurant for more than five years. They love him there. I have thanked the various managers as they've changed over the years many times, and one of the managers told me, "Carl, my whole staff interacts better when Jimmy is here. We couldn't run this place without Jimmy."

Now our community has more than forty other employers hiring the handicapped. Anderson has nine group homes and services infants to adults. Jackie would have probably told me, "Carl, now that's progress."

Jackie must have felt accepted like Jimmy did when he was voted MVP in 1949. We all benefited from Jackie, and he helped us all understand ourselves and each other better. I often told Jackie that, yes, he had helped his race, but he helped mine more.

Baseball was an interesting stage because in baseball you knew who the enemies were: the Phillies, the Giants, the Reds, the Cubs. Each team had its archrival. Each team knew the opposition. But in society, comments were sometimes made out in the open, and then Jackie knew where he stood with that person. However, the more dangerous experiences, as Jackie told me, occurred when he didn't know the opposition. Sometimes those closest to the game kept their bigoted feelings to themselves. At times we'd be at a school and we'd look around at the educators, the children, the principal, and we didn't know, with certainty, who was a friend or foe of Jimmy because openly everyone smiled. We remarked that we thought all the smiles and kind comments were genuine.

Jackie and Jimmy represent those who have changed our lives for the better. We are more sensitive—a more caring society—because of them. We have enriched ourselves by not rejecting but rather including those who are seemingly different, only to find out we are all in need of being treated with dignity.

Jackie was an athlete, not a teacher, but what I learned from him can't be taught in a classroom. It has to be taught in real life. It has to be observed, felt, lived with, and embraced.

I miss Jackie. I miss his high spirit. I miss his "never say die" attitude. I miss his tenacity. He had a gentle strength. But I think of him and I thank him when I see Jimmy and others achieve. Jackie and Jimmy, my two best buddies, changed the way we see each other, and society should be commended in the end for its inclusion.

Epilogue
The Legacy of Number 42

"Resolve to be tender with the young, compassionate with the aged, sympathetic with the striving, and tolerant with the weak and wrong, because sometime in your life you will have been all of these."

—ANONYMOUS

"**O**UR WHOLE COUNTRY BENEFITED from Jackie Robinson and his sacrifice," Hall of Famer Joe Morgan said during a 2004 ESPN telecast on "Sunday Night Baseball." I couldn't have said it better myself.

Jackie's greatest legacy was his unbelievable self-control and how that self-control paved the way for others to lead great lives. Civil rights got a fresh start with Robinson and transformed the rest of society. Baseball forced America to reevaluate itself and its practices, and in turn proved itself to be more than a game. It showed us that sometimes our national pastime can teach us a thing or two, rather than we as a society shaping our national pastime.

Jackie Robinson was a high-spirited, self-confident, militant man as well as a high achiever who resented being considered second class. His understanding of the major goal of his experience— and that the goal was bigger than him or his personal feelings —allowed him to control his anger and suppress his instinct to retaliate.

He believed in Branch Rickey and Rickey's idea that only a passive response to the indignities and hatred of the times was the right formula. It was this self-control during his first two years that made everything work, and after Rickey's gag order was lifted, responses gushed out of Jackie like a geyser. He was caustic and defensive when he needed to be, and when he went off sometimes and I'd ask him about whether it made him feel better, he responded, "Carl, I just can't let that stuff pass." I understood.

He believed in America—"America the Beautiful" the way Ray Charles sang it. He believed in an America that was united as one —not one united as a white America. I learned patience from Jackie. If he could be patient at times over civil rights, I could be patient about trivial things happening in my own life. I learned how to be a better player and a better man from Jackie. I learned the importance of good friendship. I learned the importance of speaking one's mind even in the face of criticism.

It's incomprehensible to estimate the number of lives Jackie saved through his public speaking engagements at inner-city schools. The countless hours he spent at youth clinics and youth tournaments giving encouragement to other people's children do not appear in a baseball bio or stat sheet. Kids played baseball and stayed off the streets because of Jackie. Lives turned out positive because of Jackie. Men became men because of Jackie. And through all of this Jackie felt not only happy to be a part of it but an obligation as a famous athlete to do it. He said it was "a calling."

Jackie Robinson is an American hero, an icon. Textbooks used in classrooms around the globe bear his stories. His name lives on through the ballplayers today, and his retired number 42 is honored throughout baseball.

Jackie Robinson is an important part of American history, and in that regard he has saved the Brooklyn Dodgers from fading into oblivion, for we all will be remembered as teammates of Jackie.

Our team will live on because of him, and the players will still play. And the great political and social question has been answered.

Are we better off than in centuries past when the handicapped, the different, were called misfits?

Whole families withdrew from life because of feelings of shame or guilt. The "different" were made fun of, taunted, and made to feel insignificant.

Betty and I used to see odd glances and hear snickers when Jimmy would go out with us, and now Jimmy is smiled at whenever we're in public. He's even spoken to and embraced. Just as Jackie was cheered in stands when he stole home, Jimmy is recognized as a tender person made to give love, a person to be loved, and someone with a sense of love for life.

Just looking at mainstream America, the great question is easily answered. Whether it's in the political arena, the sports arena, the business world, the entertainment world, or the educational system, our America now is a true mix of human diversity.

There's a song in the famous Broadway show *South Pacific* that says you've got to be carefully taught—taught prejudice, that is, because we are all by nature accepting and loving. Jackie and Jimmy have helped us connect with that innate good nature. We're a better society for it.

The lion has lain down by the lamb.

Yes. We are a better world because Jackie Robinson rose to the challenge and literally gave his life for it.

The bitter, just as Jackie told Newk that day in St. Louis, has been made better!

Index